Cyber Security Risk Management

ALTIORA
EST. · PUBLICATIONS · 1931

A University Level Course with Workshop Exercises

David Tuffley PhD

A comprehensive coverage of the cybersecurity standards, frameworks and operational procedures covering risk management. It is a course primarily for cybersecurity professionals but may also be of interest to professionals from related disciplines.

ISBN: 9798323933891

1st **Edition Published 2024 by Altiora Publications**

CONTENTS

INTRODUCTION TO CYBER SECURITY STANDARDS & FRAMEWORKS

HELLO & WELCOME

Organizations today face an increasing array of cyber threats that can compromise sensitive data, disrupt operations, and erode customer trust. To combat these risks, industry-recognized cyber security standards and frameworks have emerged as essential tools for establishing robust security practices and fostering a culture of cyber resilience.

This course will equip you with a thorough understanding of the most widely adopted cyber security standards and frameworks. Through ten modules, you will gain invaluable insights into risk management strategies, information security management systems, and the implementation of effective security controls.

We begin with an introduction to the purpose and structure of cyber security standards, emphasizing the importance of aligning organizational practices with industry best practices. We explore risk management frameworks, including NIST RMF and ISO 31000, which provide guidance on identifying, assessing, and mitigating risks to your organization's critical assets.

Building upon this foundation, we will investigate the intricacies of Information Security Management Systems (ISMS), with a focus on the globally recognized ISO 27001/27002 standards. This module will empower you to establish robust ISMS processes, implement security controls, and foster a culture of continuous improvement within your organization.

As we progress through the course, we will gain a comprehensive understanding of widely adopted cyber security frameworks, such as NIST CSF, NIST SP 800-53, and CIS Critical Security Controls. These frameworks offer a structured approach to identifying and mitigating cyber risks, enabling you to map security controls to your organization's unique requirements.

In addition to these overarching frameworks, the course explores specialized domains, including identity and access management, data protection and privacy, network and application security, and security operations and incident response. We delve into best practices for authentication, authorization, encryption, data privacy compliance, network segmentation, web application security, secure coding, and incident response planning.

We recognize the challenges faced by critical infrastructure and regulated industries, dedicating a module to sector-specific security standards and frameworks. This includes guidelines from NERC CIP, SOCI, AESCSF, FISMA, HIPAA, ASD Essential 8, ASD ISM, NIST SP 800-171, PCI DSS, and the Zero Trust Security Executive Order 14028.

Lastly, the course culminates with an exploration of cybersecurity capability maturity models, such as C2M2 and the Essential Eight Maturity Model. This module also covers career paths, certifications, ethical principles, and professional development opportunities in the cyber security field, equipping you with the tools to navigate and thrive in this dynamic industry.

ACKNOWLEDGEMENT OF SOURCES

Key sources that used to develop the content for this cyber security standards and frameworks course:

1. NIST Cybersecurity Framework (https://www.nist.gov/cyberframework)
2. NIST Risk Management Framework (RMF) (https://csrc.nist.gov/Projects/risk-management/rmf-overview)
3. NIST Special Publication 800-53 Security and Privacy Controls (https://csrc.nist.gov/publications/detail/sp/800-53/rev-5/final)
4. ISO/IEC 27001 Information Security Management Systems (https://www.iso.org/isoiec-27001-information-security.html)
5. ISO 31000 Risk Management Standard (https://www.iso.org/iso-31000-risk-management.html)
6. CIS Critical Security Controls (https://www.cisecurity.org/controls)
7. OWASP Top 10 Web Application Security Risks (https://owasp.org/www-project-top-ten/)
1. 10. ASD Essential Eight Maturity Model (https://www.cyber.gov.au/acsc/view-all-content/essential-eight)
2. 11. GDPR (General Data Protection Regulation) (https://gdpr.eu/)
3. 12. HIPAA Security Rule (https://www.hhs.gov/hipaa/for-professionals/security/index.html)
4. 13. FISMA (Federal Information Security Modernization Act) (https://www.cisa.gov/federal-information-security-modernization-act)
5. 14. Payment Card Industry Data Security Standard (PCI DSS) (https://www.pcisecuritystandards.org/)
6. 15. Executive Order 14028 on Improving the Nation's Cybersecurity (https://www.whitehouse.gov/briefing-room/presidential-actions/2021/05/12/executive-order-on-improving-the-nations-cybersecurity/)

This list covers the key standards, frameworks, regulations and guidance from authoritative bodies like NIST, ISO, CIS, OWASP, NERC, ASD, EU, HHS, CISA and the PCI Council that are referenced in the course modules. Additional sector-specific standards and published cybersecurity career roadmaps were likely consulted as well.

HOW SHOULD YOU APPROACH THIS COURSE?

The course is arranged in modules that we recommend you do each week, without skipping weeks with the intention of catching up later. Good time management is key ingredient if professional practice and we strongly encourage it in this course.

The first thing to do is download the self-contained course notes in PDF for online consumption. A printed copy is also available from Amazon for a fee, but you do not necessarily need to have the printed book, only if you want it.

Go through each module, listening / watching the material and read the content as well as stay up to date with any assessment tasks mentioned there.

For in-person students and those enrolled in the online synchronous offering, try to attend the online lectures and in-person workshops each week. These are recorded for your later viewing if the timing of the scheduled event is awkward. You will get the most from this course if you invest your time and effort in making the learning journey.

For students enrolled in the fully asynchronous mode, you have no deadlines apart from the Trimester start and finish dates. It's important that you manage your time well and work your way through the content for a satisfaction finish. You are encouraged to interact with the other students on the forums provided.

MODULE 1.
INTRODUCTION TO CYBER SECURITY STANDARDS & FRAMEWORKS

Module Summary: This module provides a comprehensive introduction to cybersecurity standards and frameworks, emphasizing their significance in establishing and maintaining a robust security posture. It explores the purpose and structure of these guidelines, underscoring the importance of aligning organizational practices with recognized standards to mitigate cyber risks and ensure business continuity.

The module goes into the overarching principles and concepts that form the foundation of cybersecurity standards, such as the CIA triad, defence-in-depth strategies, and secure system development lifecycles. It highlights renowned frameworks like NIST's Cybersecurity Framework, ISO/IEC 27000 series, and sector-specific standards tailored to critical infrastructure and regulated industries.

The module also emphasizes the legal and regulatory drivers that necessitate adherence to established cybersecurity benchmarks. It discusses how aligning with these standards facilitates compliance with laws and regulations, such as HIPAA, PCI DSS, and GDPR, while mitigating the risks of non-compliance and fostering trust with stakeholders and customers.

1.1 OVERVIEW OF CYBER SECURITY STANDARDS AND FRAMEWORKS

Cyber security standards and frameworks provide a structured approach to managing and mitigating cyber risks within organizations. These guidelines offer comprehensive sets of best practices, controls, and processes designed to protect critical assets and ensure business continuity.

At the core of these standards and frameworks lie well-defined security principles and concepts. These include the CIA triad (Confidentiality, Integrity, and Availability), defence-in-depth strategies, least privilege access, and secure system development lifecycles. By adhering to these principles, organizations can build robust security postures tailored to their specific needs and risk landscapes.

Several renowned bodies, such as the *National Institute of Standards and Technology* (NIST), the *International Organization for Standardization* (ISO), and the *Centre for Internet Security* (CIS), have developed widely adopted cyber security standards and frameworks. NIST's *Cybersecurity Framework* (CSF) and Special Publication 800-53 provide a comprehensive set of security controls and guidelines for organizations to manage cyber risks. The ISO/IEC 27000 series, including ISO 27001 and 27002, offers a systematic approach to establishing, implementing, and maintaining an Information Security Management System (ISMS).

In addition to these overarching frameworks, sector-specific standards have emerged to address the unique security challenges faced by critical infrastructure and regulated industries. Examples include the NERC Critical Infrastructure Protection (CIP) standards for the energy sector, the HIPAA Security Rule for healthcare organizations, and the Payment Card Industry Data Security Standard (PCI DSS) for businesses handling payment card data.

These standards and frameworks are designed to be flexible and adaptable, allowing organizations to tailor the implementation to their specific needs, risk profiles, and regulatory requirements. They provide a common language and set of guidelines for organizations to communicate and collaborate with stakeholders, partners, and regulatory bodies.

By adopting and adhering to these cyber security standards and frameworks, organizations can establish a robust security posture, enhance their ability to detect and respond to cyber threats, and demonstrate compliance with relevant laws and regulations. Ultimately, these guidelines serve as invaluable resources for organizations seeking to protect their digital assets, maintain business continuity, and foster trust with customers and partners.

1.2 PURPOSE AND STRUCTURE OF SECURITY STANDARDS

Security standards serve as comprehensive guidelines designed to help organizations establish, implement, and maintain effective security practices. These standards are developed by recognized bodies and experts in the field of cybersecurity, drawing upon years of research, best practices, and lessons learned from real-world incidents.

The primary purpose of security standards is to provide a uniform set of principles, controls, and processes that organizations can adopt to mitigate risks, protect their critical assets, and ensure business continuity. By adhering to these standards, organizations can strengthen their overall security posture, foster a culture of security awareness, and demonstrate compliance with relevant laws and regulations.

Security standards are typically structured in a hierarchical manner, with different levels of specificity and granularity. At the highest level, the standards outline overarching security principles, such as the CIA triad (Confidentiality, Integrity, and Availability), risk management strategies, and governance frameworks.

Beneath this foundational layer, the standards delve into specific security domains, such as access control, cryptography, physical security, incident response, and business continuity planning. Within each domain, the standards provide detailed guidance on implementing security controls, procedures, and best practices.

For example, the widely adopted ISO/IEC 27001 standard is structured around the concept of an Information Security Management System (ISMS), which encompasses a comprehensive set of policies, processes, and controls for managing information security risks. The standard outlines the requirements for establishing, implementing, monitoring, and continually improving an ISMS within an organization.

Similarly, the NIST Cybersecurity Framework (CSF) is organized around five core functions. Identify, Protect, Detect, Respond, and Recover. Each function includes a set of categories and subcategories that provide guidance on specific security activities and desired outcomes.

Security standards often include annexes, appendices, and reference materials that provide additional resources, such as control catalogs, implementation guides, and sector-specific guidelines. These supplementary materials aid organizations in tailoring the standard's implementation to their unique requirements and risk profiles.

By adhering to the purpose and structure of security standards, organizations can establish a comprehensive and systematic approach to managing cybersecurity risks, ensuring compliance with regulations, and fostering a culture of security awareness throughout their operations.

1.3 IMPORTANCE OF ALIGNING SECURITY PRACTICES WITH STANDARDS

Aligning an organization's security practices with recognized standards is of paramount importance. Failure to adhere to these guidelines can leave organizations vulnerable to costly data breaches, operational disruptions, and reputational damage.

Adopting industry-accepted security standards ensures that an organization's security measures are comprehensive, up-to-date, and aligned with best practices. These standards are developed by subject matter experts and reflect the collective knowledge and experience of the cybersecurity community. By aligning practices with these standards, organizations can benefit from a well-defined and proven approach to managing cyber risks.

Implementing security controls and processes outlined in standards such as ISO 27001, NIST CSF, and CIS Controls helps organizations establish a strong security posture. These guidelines cover a wide range of areas, including access control, incident response, risk management, and security awareness training. Adhering to these standards ensures that critical aspects of security are not overlooked, reducing the likelihood of successful cyber-attacks.

Moreover, aligning with security standards facilitates better communication and collaboration within an organization and with external stakeholders. These standards provide a common language and framework, enabling effective coordination among different departments, vendors, and partners. This alignment fosters a shared understanding of security objectives and responsibilities, leading to more cohesive and efficient security efforts.

Compliance with security standards is often a requirement for organizations operating in regulated industries or handling sensitive data. By aligning practices with standards such as HIPAA, PCI DSS, or NERC CIP, organizations can demonstrate their commitment to protecting sensitive information and critical infrastructure, reducing the risk of penalties and legal liabilities.

Furthermore, adopting security standards can enhance an organization's reputation and foster trust with customers, partners, and stakeholders. Demonstrating adherence to recognized standards signals a commitment to security and a proactive approach to risk management, which can provide a competitive advantage in today's security-conscious business environment.

1.4 LEGAL AND REGULATORY COMPLIANCE

Organizations face a complex web of legal and regulatory requirements when it comes to protecting sensitive data and critical systems. Failure to comply with these laws and regulations can result in severe consequences, including hefty fines, legal liabilities, and reputational damage. Aligning with widely recognized cybersecurity standards and frameworks is crucial for demonstrating compliance and mitigating risks associated with non-compliance.

Numerous laws and regulations mandate the implementation of specific security controls and practices. For instance, the Health Insurance Portability and Accountability Act (HIPAA) in the United States outlines strict requirements for protecting the privacy and security of health information. Healthcare organizations must adhere to the HIPAA Security Rule by implementing measures such as access controls, risk assessments, and incident response procedures.

Similarly, the Payment Card Industry Data Security Standard (PCI DSS) is a set of requirements designed to ensure the secure handling of payment card data. Any organization that processes, stores, or transmits cardholder data must comply with PCI DSS to maintain a secure environment and prevent data breaches.

In the realm of critical infrastructure, the North American Electric Reliability Corporation (NERC) has established Critical Infrastructure Protection (CIP) standards to secure the bulk electric system. These standards are mandatory for electric utilities and other entities involved in the generation, transmission, and distribution of electricity.

Beyond industry-specific regulations, there are broader legal frameworks that organizations must consider. The General Data Protection Regulation (GDPR) in the European Union sets stringent rules for the collection, processing, protection of personal data, impacting any organization that handles EU citizens' data.

Aligning with widely adopted cybersecurity standards and frameworks, such as the NIST Cybersecurity Framework (CSF), ISO 27001, and CIS Controls, can greatly facilitate compliance with these legal and regulatory requirements. These standards provide comprehensive guidance on implementing robust security controls, risk management processes, and governance structures, which directly address many of the mandates outlined in various laws and regulations.

By leveraging the security controls and best practices prescribed by these standards, organizations can streamline their compliance efforts, reduce the risk of non-compliance, and demonstrate their commitment to protecting sensitive data and critical systems.

1.5 WORKSHOP EXERCISE:
INTRODUCTION TO CYBERSECURITY STANDARDS & FRAMEWORKS

Workshop Exercise - Security Standards and Frameworks

Scenario: You are a cybersecurity consultant recently hired by a fast-growing e-commerce company. The company has experienced a significant increase in customer traffic and online sales in recent months. However, they lack a formal cybersecurity strategy and are unsure how to best protect their growing digital assets and customer data.

Task: Following the principles covered in *Module 1: Introduction to Cybersecurity Standards & Frameworks*, recommend a suitable cybersecurity framework for the e-commerce company.

Your recommendation should address the following aspects (a paragraph for each point):

1. Framework Selection:

1. Briefly analyse the specific needs and risk profile of the e-commerce company (consider factors like the type of data they handle, size of the organization, and industry regulations).
2. Briefly compare prominent cybersecurity frameworks like NIST Cybersecurity Framework (CSF), ISO/IEC 27001, and CIS Controls.
3. Justify your selection of a specific framework based on its suitability for the e-commerce company's context.

2. Framework Implementation:

1. Briefly outline a high-level plan for implementing the chosen framework within the e-commerce company.

2. Consider key steps such as conducting a risk assessment, identifying relevant security controls, and establishing an implementation roadmap.
3. Benefits and Challenges:

Deliverables:

A written report of approximately 400 words within the Workshop document.

Ensure your report has clear headings for each section (Framework Selection, Implementation, Benefits & Challenges).

Avoid directly copying and pasting information from online sources. Utilize the knowledge gained from Module 1 to Analyse the scenario and propose a solution tailored to the e-commerce company. You can leverage online resources to research specific frameworks and best practices but remember to paraphrase and avoid plagiarism.

This workshop exercise will help you reinforce your understanding of cybersecurity frameworks, assess their applicability in real-world scenarios, and develop a strategic approach to implementing security best practices within an organization.

NOTES

MODULE 2.
RISK MANAGEMENT FRAMEWORKS

Module Summary. The module covers important risk management frameworks that provide structured approaches for identifying, assessing, and mitigating risks within organizations.

It examines the NIST Risk Management Framework (RMF), which offers a comprehensive 7-step process for integrating security and risk management activities into an organization's systems and operations. The RMF emphasizes continuous monitoring and risk assessment.

The module also discusses the ISO 31000 standard, an internationally recognized framework that provides principles, guidelines, and a generic process for risk management across all types of organizations. It promotes integrating risk practices into decision-making processes.

Risk identification, assessment, and treatment are covered as critical components for proactively identifying threats, analysing likelihood and impact, and implementing appropriate mitigations. Both qualitative and quantitative risk assessment methods are explained.

Vulnerability management is highlighted as a crucial process for identifying, evaluating, prioritizing, and remediating vulnerabilities in systems and applications to reduce exploitation risks.

Finally, the module examines third-party risk management (TPRM), which focuses on identifying, assessing, and mitigating risks associated with using third-party vendors, suppliers, and service providers through due diligence, contracts, monitoring, and offboarding processes.

2.1 NIST RISK MANAGEMENT FRAMEWORK (RMF)

The NIST Risk Management Framework (RMF) is a comprehensive process designed to help organizations manage information security risks across their systems and operations. Developed by the National Institute of Standards and Technology (NIST), the RMF provides a disciplined, structured, and flexible approach to integrating security and risk management activities into an organization's enterprise architecture and system development life cycle processes.

At its core, the RMF is a seven-step process that encompasses the entire risk management lifecycle. The steps include preparing for the execution of the RMF, categorizing the system and information based on impact levels, selecting appropriate security controls, implementing those controls, assessing their effectiveness, authorizing the system for operation, and continuously monitoring the security posture.

One of the key strengths of the RMF is its emphasis on continuous monitoring and ongoing risk assessment. Rather than treating risk management as a one-time activity, the framework encourages organizations to continuously monitor their security posture, assess changes in the risk environment, and adapt their security controls accordingly.

The RMF also provides a comprehensive catalog of security controls, known as NIST Special Publication 800-53, which covers a wide range of security domains, including access control, incident response, system and communications protection, and risk assessment. These controls are designed to be tailored to the specific needs and risk profiles of different organizations and systems.

By adopting the NIST RMF, organizations can establish a robust and repeatable process for managing information security risks, ensuring compliance with relevant laws and regulations, and fostering a culture of risk awareness throughout their operations. The framework's flexibility and scalability make it applicable to organizations of various sizes and sectors, from small businesses to large enterprises and government agencies.

2.2 ISO 31000 RISK MANAGEMENT STANDARD

The ISO 31000 is an internationally recognized standard that provides principles, guidelines, and a generic process for risk management. Developed by the International Organization for Standardization (ISO), this standard offers a systematic and comprehensive approach to identifying, analyzing, evaluating, and addressing risks faced by organizations of all types and sizes.

At its core, the ISO 31000 standard emphasizes the integration of risk management practices into an organization's overall management system and decision-making processes. It promotes a structured and iterative approach to risk management, enabling organizations to continually identify, assess, and respond to potential risks in a proactive and effective manner.

The standard outlines a series of principles that should guide risk management efforts, such as continual improvement, human and cultural factors, and the inclusion of stakeholder perspectives. These principles serve as a foundation for establishing a robust risk management framework within an organization.

The ISO 31000 also defines a clear risk management process, which includes steps such as establishing the context, risk identification, risk analysis, risk evaluation, risk treatment, monitoring and review, and communication and consultation. This process provides a structured methodology for organizations to systematically identify and address risks across all areas of their operations.

One of the key strengths of the ISO 31000 standard is its versatility and scalability. It can be applied to various types of risks, including strategic, operational, financial, and compliance risks, among others. Additionally, the standard is designed to be adaptable to different organizational contexts, allowing organizations to tailor the risk management approach to their specific needs and circumstances.

By adopting the ISO 31000 standard, organizations can foster a risk-aware culture, make informed decisions based on a comprehensive understanding of risks, and ultimately improve their overall resilience and performance.

2.3 RISK IDENTIFICATION, ASSESSMENT, AND TREATMENT

Risk identification, assessment, and treatment are critical components of an effective risk management program. These interconnected processes enable organizations to proactively identify potential threats, analyse their likelihood and impact, and implement appropriate measures to mitigate or manage those risks.

Risk identification involves systematically identifying and documenting risks that could potentially impact an organization's objectives, operations, or assets. This process can involve techniques such as brainstorming sessions, risk checklists, process analysis, and stakeholder consultations. Effective risk identification ensures that all relevant risks are accounted for and addressed.

Once risks have been identified, risk assessment is the next step. This process involves analyzing the identified risks to determine their potential consequences and the likelihood of their occurrence. Risk assessment helps organizations prioritize risks based on their severity and potential impact, allowing them to allocate resources effectively and make informed decisions.

Qualitative and quantitative methods can be used for risk assessment, depending on the nature of the risks and the availability of data. Qualitative assessments rely on subjective evaluations and descriptive scales, while quantitative assessments involve numerical data and statistical analysis.

Following risk assessment, organizations must determine appropriate risk treatment strategies. These strategies can include risk avoidance (eliminating the risk source), risk mitigation (implementing controls to reduce the risk), risk transfer (sharing or transferring the risk to a third party), or risk acceptance (acknowledging and monitoring the risk).

The selection of risk treatment strategies should be based on factors such as the organization's risk appetite, available resources, legal or regulatory requirements, and the potential costs and benefits of each strategy.

Effective risk identification, assessment, and treatment are ongoing processes that require regular monitoring and review. As the risk landscape evolves, organizations must continuously identify new risks, reassess existing risks, and adapt their treatment strategies accordingly.

2.4 VULNERABILITY MANAGEMENT

Vulnerability management is a critical process that involves identifying, evaluating, prioritizing, and mitigating vulnerabilities within an organization's systems, applications, and networks. Vulnerabilities are weaknesses or flaws that can be exploited by cyber threats, potentially leading to data breaches, system compromises, or other security incidents.

Effective vulnerability management begins with vulnerability discovery. This involves using various techniques and tools to scan systems and applications for known vulnerabilities. Sources of vulnerability information include vendor advisories, security databases, penetration testing, and threat intelligence feeds.

Once vulnerabilities are identified, they must be analysed and prioritized based on factors such as the potential impact, likelihood of exploitation, and the criticality of the affected assets. This risk-based approach ensures that resources are focused on addressing the most significant vulnerabilities first.

Vulnerability remediation is the next step in the process. This can involve applying software patches, implementing configuration changes, deploying compensating controls, or upgrading to newer versions of software or hardware that are not affected by the vulnerability.

It is crucial to have a well-defined process for testing and deploying vulnerability remediation measures, as poorly implemented fixes can introduce new issues or disrupt system operations. Change management procedures and thorough testing in non-production environments are essential to ensure a smooth and secure remediation process.

Vulnerability management is an ongoing process that requires continuous monitoring and assessment. New vulnerabilities are constantly being discovered, and the threat landscape is ever-evolving. Organizations should establish a regular cadence for vulnerability scans, risk assessments, and remediation activities to maintain a robust security posture.

Effective vulnerability management not only helps organizations mitigate potential risks but also demonstrates compliance with industry standards and regulatory requirements, such as those mandated by PCI DSS, HIPAA, or NIST frameworks.

2.5 THIRD-PARTY RISK MANAGEMENT (TPRM)

Third-Party Risk Management (TPRM) is a critical process that focuses on identifying, assessing, and mitigating risks associated with the use of third-party vendors, suppliers, and service providers. As organizations increasingly rely on external partners for various services and products, they become exposed to potential risks that can impact their operations, security, and compliance posture.

TPRM involves a comprehensive approach to managing the entire lifecycle of third-party relationships, from due diligence and selection to ongoing monitoring and termination. It begins with a thorough evaluation of potential third parties, assessing their security practices, data handling procedures, and overall risk profile.

During the evaluation phase, organizations may conduct risk assessments, review security policies and controls, perform on-site audits, and request evidence of compliance with relevant standards and regulations. This due diligence process helps organizations make informed decisions about which third parties to engage with and under what conditions.

Once a third party is selected, robust contracts and service level agreements (SLAs) should be established to clearly define security and privacy requirements, data handling practices, incident response procedures, and responsibilities of both parties.

Ongoing monitoring is a crucial aspect of TPRM, as third-party risks can evolve over time. This involves regular security reviews, vulnerability assessments, and continuous monitoring of the third party's security posture. Effective communication channels and incident reporting processes should be in place to ensure timely response to any identified risks or security incidents.

When terminating a third-party relationship, organizations must carefully manage the offboarding process, ensuring that sensitive data is securely returned or properly disposed of, and access to systems and resources is revoked promptly.

By implementing a robust TPRM program, organizations can better manage the risks associated with third-party relationships, maintain regulatory compliance, and protect their sensitive data and intellectual property from potential threats or breaches introduced by external partners.

2.6 WORKSHOP EXERCISE: RISK MANAGEMENT FRAMEWORKS

Workshop Exercise - Risk Management in Action

Scenario: You are a cybersecurity consultant engaged by a cloud-based file storage service provider. The company has recently experienced a significant increase in customer accounts and data storage volume. While they have basic security measures in place, they recognize the need for a more structured approach to managing cybersecurity risks associated with their cloud storage platform.

Task: Following the principles covered in *Module 2: Risk Management Frameworks*, recommend a suitable risk management framework for the cloud storage service provider.

Your recommendation should address the following aspects (a paragraph for each point):

1. Framework Selection:

1. Briefly analyse the specific needs and risk profile of the cloud storage service provider (consider factors like the type of data they store, security measures in place, and regulatory compliance requirements).
2. Compare prominent risk management frameworks like NIST RMF and ISO 31000.
3. Justify your selection of a specific framework based on its suitability for the cloud storage provider's context.

2. Benefits and Challenges:

1. Discuss the potential benefits of adopting a risk management framework for the cloud storage service provider.
2. Consider benefits such as improved security posture, enhanced customer trust, and streamlined compliance efforts.
3. Acknowledge potential challenges associated with framework implementation, such as resource allocation and cultural change.

Deliverables:

A written report of approximately 400 words within the Workshop document.

Ensure your report has clear headings for each section (Framework Selection, Benefits & Challenges).

Avoid directly copying and pasting information from online sources. Utilize the knowledge gained from Module 2 to Analyse the scenario and propose a solution tailored to the cloud storage service provider. You can leverage online resources to research specific frameworks and best practices but remember to paraphrase and avoid plagiarism.

This workshop exercise will help you reinforce your understanding of applying risk management frameworks in a real-world scenario. You will develop a plan to identify, assess, and mitigate risks associated with a cloud storage platform, ensuring the security of sensitive customer data.

NOTES

MODULE 3.
INFORMATION SECURITY MANAGEMENT SYSTEMS (ISMS)

Module Summary. This module provides an overview of the ISO 27001/27002 standards for establishing and maintaining an Information Security Management System (ISMS). It emphasizes the importance of a systematic approach to managing information security risks through the Plan-Do-Check-Act (PDCA) cycle.

Key aspects covered include defining the scope and policy, conducting risk assessments, implementing security controls from the ISO 27002 guidelines, establishing supporting processes, and continuous improvement through monitoring and review. Implementing an effective ISMS involves selecting and tailoring controls, designing policies and procedures, deploying controls, testing, and ongoing monitoring.

Risk treatment strategies, such as risk avoidance, mitigation, transfer, or acceptance, are crucial for addressing identified risks. Continuous improvement, monitoring, and adapting to evolving threats and business needs are fundamental principles for maintaining a robust and resilient ISMS.

3.1 ISO 27001/27002 – INFORMATION SECURITY MANAGEMENT SYSTEM

The ISO 27001 and ISO 27002 standards are part of the ISO/IEC 27000 family of standards, which provide a comprehensive framework for establishing, implementing, maintaining, and continually improving an Information Security Management System (ISMS). These standards are widely adopted globally and serve as a benchmark for organizations seeking to protect their information assets and ensure the confidentiality, integrity, and availability of their data.

ISO 27001 is the main standard that specifies the requirements for an ISMS. It outlines a systematic approach to managing information security risks, covering all aspects of an organization's operations, including people, processes, and technology. The standard is designed to be applicable to organizations of all sizes and across various industries.

At the core of ISO 27001 is the Plan-Do-Check-Act (PDCA) cycle, which promotes a continuous improvement approach to information security management. This iterative process involves planning and establishing the ISMS, implementing, and operating the necessary controls, monitoring and reviewing the effectiveness of the ISMS, and making adjustments or improvements as needed.

The standard requires organizations to define an information security policy, conduct risk assessments, select appropriate security controls from the ISO 27002 control set, and implement these controls through documented policies, procedures, and processes. It also emphasizes the importance of management commitment, resource allocation, and regular internal audits and management reviews.

ISO 27002, on the other hand, is a code of practice that provides guidelines and recommendations for implementing the security controls outlined in ISO 27001. It covers a wide range of security domains, including access control, cryptography, physical and environmental security, operations security, communications security, and information security incident management.

Together, ISO 27001 and ISO 27002 provide a comprehensive framework for organizations to establish, maintain, and continually improve their information security management practices. By adopting these standards, organizations can:

1. Protect their information assets from potential threats and vulnerabilities.
2. Ensure compliance with legal, regulatory, and contractual requirements.
3. Enhance their overall security posture and resilience.
4. Gain a competitive advantage by demonstrating a commitment to information security.
5. Foster a culture of security awareness and responsibility throughout the organization.

Implementing an ISMS based on the ISO 27001/27002 standards requires a significant investment of time and resources, but the benefits of a robust and comprehensive information security management system are invaluable in today's increasingly complex and threat-laden digital landscape.

3.2 ESTABLISHING AN ISMS

Establishing an effective Information Security Management System (ISMS) is a critical step for organizations seeking to protect their information assets and maintain compliance with the ISO 27001 standard. This process involves a structured approach that spans several key phases.

The first phase is to define the scope and boundaries of the ISMS. Organizations must clearly identify the information assets, processes, and systems that will be covered by the ISMS, as well as any relevant legal, regulatory, or contractual requirements that must be addressed.

Next, organizations must gain leadership commitment and establish an information security policy. Top management support is crucial for ensuring the necessary resources and authority are allocated to the ISMS implementation. The information security policy should outline the organization's overall approach to managing information security risks and align with its business objectives.

A comprehensive risk assessment is then conducted to identify potential threats, vulnerabilities, and their associated impacts on the organization's information assets. This risk assessment serves as the foundation for selecting and implementing appropriate security controls from the ISO 27001 Annex A control set.

The selection and implementation of security controls are central to the ISMS. These controls cover various domains such as access control, cryptography, physical security, operational security, and incident management. Organizations must document and communicate the implemented controls through policies, procedures, and operational guidelines.

Establishing an ISMS also requires the development of supporting processes and documentation. This includes processes for risk management, change management, incident response, and continual improvement. Additionally, organizations must define roles and responsibilities, provide security awareness training, and establish metrics for measuring the effectiveness of the ISMS.

Once the ISMS is established, organizations must conduct internal audits and management reviews to assess its performance and identify areas for improvement. This iterative process helps organizations maintain compliance with the ISO 27001 standard and continually enhance their information security posture.

Establishing an ISMS is not a one-time effort but rather an ongoing commitment to managing information security risks. By following the structured approach outlined in ISO 27001, organizations can develop a robust and comprehensive ISMS that protects their valuable information assets and fosters a culture of security within their operations.

3,3 IMPLEMENTING SECURITY CONTROLS AND PROCESSES

Implementing effective security controls and processes is at the heart of an organization's Information Security Management System (ISMS) based on the ISO 27001 standard. These controls and processes are designed to mitigate identified risks and protect the confidentiality, integrity, and availability of the organization's information assets.

The ISO 27001 Annex A provides a comprehensive set of 114 security controls, spanning 14 domains such as access control, cryptography, physical security, operations security, and incident management. Organizations must carefully select and tailor these controls to address their specific risk landscape and operational requirements.

Implementing security controls involves a structured approach that typically includes the following steps:

1. Security control selection. Based on the risk assessment and treatment plan, organizations identify the relevant controls from Annex A that address their specific risks.

2. Control implementation planning. Detailed implementation plans are developed, outlining the specific actions, resources, responsibilities, and timelines for implementing each selected control.

3. Control design and documentation. Organizations design and document the policies, procedures, and processes that govern the implementation and operation of the selected controls.

4. Control implementation and deployment. The designed controls are implemented and deployed across the relevant systems, processes, and organizational units.

5. Control testing and validation. Implemented controls are thoroughly tested and validated to ensure they are operating as intended and effectively mitigating the identified risks.

6. Control monitoring and review. Continuous monitoring and periodic reviews are conducted to assess the effectiveness of the implemented controls and identify any necessary adjustments or improvements.

In addition to implementing technical controls, organizations must also establish supporting processes and procedures as part of their ISMS. These processes may include risk management, change management, incident response, business continuity planning, and security awareness and training programs.

Effective implementation of security controls and processes requires collaboration across different departments and functions within the organization. It also necessitates clear communication, comprehensive documentation, and regular training and awareness programs to ensure that all employees understand and adhere to the established security practices.

By diligently implementing and maintaining the required security controls and processes, organizations can achieve a robust ISMS that addresses their unique risk landscape, meets regulatory and compliance requirements, and fosters a culture of security throughout their operations.

3.4 CONTINUOUS IMPROVEMENT AND MONITORING

Continuous improvement and monitoring are fundamental principles that underpin the effectiveness of an organization's Information Security Management System (ISMS). The ISO 27001 standard emphasizes the importance of adopting a cyclical approach to managing information security risks, fostering a culture of ongoing enhancement and adaptation.

The concept of continuous improvement is deeply rooted in the Plan-Do-Check-Act (PDCA) cycle, which serves as the foundation for the ISMS implementation and maintenance process. This iterative cycle involves:

1. Plan. Establish information security policies, objectives, processes, and procedures relevant to managing risks and improving the ISMS.

2. Do. Implement and operate the planned ISMS controls and processes.

3. Check. Monitor and review the ISMS and its controls for effectiveness, compliance, and performance against the organization's security objectives.
4. Act. Take actions to continually improve the ISMS based on the results of the monitoring and review activities.

Continuous monitoring is a crucial aspect of the "Check" phase and involves regularly assessing the ISMS's performance, vulnerabilities, and evolving threats. This can be achieved through various mechanisms, such as:

1. Regular internal audits and management reviews to evaluate the ISMS's conformity to ISO 27001 requirements and the organization's security policies.
2. Vulnerability assessments and penetration testing to identify and address potential weaknesses in systems and controls.
3. Continuous monitoring of security events, incidents, and trends through log analysis, security information and event management (SIEM) tools, and threat intelligence feeds.
4. Monitoring of legal, regulatory, and contractual requirements to ensure ongoing compliance.

The results of these monitoring activities provide valuable insights into the effectiveness of the ISMS and highlight areas for improvement. Organizations can then take corrective and preventive actions, such as updating policies and procedures, implementing additional controls, or providing further training and awareness programs.

Continuous improvement also involves regularly reviewing and updating the ISMS to reflect changes in the organization's risk landscape, business objectives, and technological advancements. This agility allows the ISMS to remain relevant and effective in protecting the organization's information assets.

By embracing the principles of continuous improvement and monitoring, organizations can maintain a robust and adaptive ISMS that proactively addresses emerging threats and evolving business needs, fostering a culture of security excellence and resilience.

3.5 RISK TREATMENT AND MITIGATION STRATEGIES

Risk treatment and mitigation strategies are essential components of an effective Information Security Management System (ISMS) based on the ISO 27001 standard. These strategies outline the approaches and actions organizations take to address identified risks and reduce their potential impact on information assets and operations.

The ISO 27001 standard provides a structured approach to risk treatment, which typically involves the following steps:

1. Risk evaluation. Analyse and prioritize risks based on their likelihood of occurrence and potential consequences, considering factors such as legal and regulatory requirements, stakeholder expectations, and the organization's risk appetite.
2. Risk treatment options. Select appropriate risk treatment options based on the evaluated risks. These options can include:
   - Risk avoidance. Eliminating the risk source or deciding not to engage in the risk-inducing activity.
   - Risk mitigation. Implementing controls and safeguards to reduce the likelihood or impact of the risk.
   - Risk transfer. Sharing or transferring a portion of the risk to third parties, such as through insurance or outsourcing arrangements.
   - Risk acceptance. Consciously accepting the risk if it aligns with the organization's risk tolerance and cannot be adequately addressed through other options.
3. Risk treatment plan. Develop a comprehensive plan that outlines the selected risk treatment options, associated actions, responsibilities, resources, and timelines for implementation.
4. Implementation and monitoring. Execute the risk treatment plan, implementing the chosen controls and mitigation strategies, and continuously monitor their effectiveness in managing the identified risks.

Common risk mitigation strategies within an ISMS may include:

- Technical controls. Implementing security solutions such as firewalls, antivirus software, access controls, encryption, and secure system configurations.
- Administrative controls. Establishing policies, procedures, awareness programs, and governance structures to manage information security risks.
- Physical controls. Implementing measures to protect physical assets, such as secure facilities, environmental controls, and equipment protection.

Effective risk treatment and mitigation strategies require a deep understanding of the organization's risk landscape, assets, and operational requirements. Regular risk assessments, continuous monitoring, and periodic reviews are necessary to ensure that the implemented strategies remain relevant and effective in addressing evolving threats and changing business needs.

By adopting a structured approach to risk treatment and mitigation, organizations can proactively address potential vulnerabilities, comply with regulatory requirements, and protect their valuable information assets, ultimately enhancing their overall security posture and resilience.

3.6 WORKSHOP EXERCISE: INFORMATION SECURITY MANAGEMENT SYSTEMS (ISMS)

Workshop Exercise - Implementing an ISMS

Scenario: You are a cybersecurity consultant recently hired by a university. The university has experienced a number of cybersecurity incidents in recent years, including data breaches involving student records and intellectual property. In response, the university leadership has recognized the need to implement a formal information security program.

Task: Following the principles covered in *Module 3: Information Security Management Systems (ISMS),* recommend a framework for establishing an ISMS for the university.

Your recommendation should address the following aspects (a paragraph for each point):

1. Framework Selection:

1. Briefly analyse the specific needs and risk profile of the university (consider factors like the type of data they handle, size and complexity of the IT environment, and regulatory compliance requirements).
2. Briefly discuss the ISO 27001 and ISO 27002 standards and their suitability for the university.
3. Justify your selection of the chosen framework.

2. Benefits and Challenges:

1. Discuss the potential benefits of adopting an ISMS for the university.
2. Consider benefits such as improved information security posture, enhanced compliance, and increased stakeholder trust.
3. Acknowledge potential challenges associated with ISMS implementation, such as resource allocation, cultural change management, and ongoing maintenance.

Deliverables:

A written report of approximately 400 words within the Workshop document.

Ensure your report has clear headings for each section (Framework Selection, Implementation, Benefits & Challenges).

Avoid directly copying and pasting information from online sources. Utilize the knowledge gained from Module 3 to Analyse the scenario and propose a solution tailored to the university. You can leverage online resources to research specific frameworks and best practices but remember to paraphrase and avoid plagiarism.

This workshop exercise will help you solidify your understanding of implementing an ISMS in a real-world educational setting. You will develop a plan to establish a systematic approach to managing information security risks at the university, protecting sensitive student data, faculty research, and critical university operations.

NOTES

Cybersecurity Risk Management

MODULE 4.
CYBER SECURITY FRAMEWORKS & CONTROLS

Module Summary. This module explores prominent cybersecurity frameworks and control sets, such as the NIST Cybersecurity Framework (NIST CSF), NIST SP 800-53 Security and Privacy Controls, and the CIS Critical Security Controls. The

NIST CSF provides a risk-based approach to cybersecurity, organized around five core functions: Identify, Protect, Detect, Respond, and Recover. NIST SP 800-53 offers a comprehensive catalogue of security and privacy controls tailored for federal information systems.

The CIS Controls focus on mitigating the most prevalent cyber threats through prioritized safeguards. The module emphasizes mapping controls to organizational requirements, ensuring alignment with risks, regulations, and business objectives. It also covers control implementation strategies, including planning, deployment, documentation, and communication.

Continuous assessment through testing, monitoring, and corrective actions is crucial for evaluating control effectiveness and maintaining a robust security posture. Effective control implementation and mapping foster a dynamic, risk-based approach to cybersecurity management.

4.1 NIST CYBERSECURITY FRAMEWORK (NIST CSF)

The NIST Cybersecurity Framework (NIST CSF) is a voluntary risk-based framework developed by the National Institute of Standards and Technology (NIST) to provide organizations with a comprehensive set of guidelines for improving their cybersecurity posture. The framework is designed to be flexible and adaptable, allowing organizations across various industries and sectors to apply it to their specific needs and risk profiles.

The NIST CSF is organized around five core functions. Identify, Protect, Detect, Respond, and Recover. These functions provide a strategic view of the lifecycle of cybersecurity risk management activities:

1. **Identify**. Develop an organizational understanding of the risks to systems, assets, data, and capabilities. This includes asset management, risk assessment, and risk management strategies.
2. **Protect**. Implement appropriate safeguards to ensure the delivery of critical infrastructure services. This includes access control, awareness and training, data security, and protective technology.
3. **Detect**. Implement appropriate activities to identify the occurrence of a cybersecurity event. This includes continuous monitoring, anomaly detection, and security continuous monitoring.

33

4. **Respond**. Develop and implement appropriate activities to take action regarding a detected cybersecurity incident. This includes response planning, communications, analysis, and mitigation.
5. **Recover**. Develop and implement appropriate activities to maintain plans for resilience and to restore any capabilities or services that were impaired due to a cybersecurity incident. This includes recovery planning, improvements, and communications.

Within each of these core functions, the NIST CSF provides categories and subcategories that describe specific cybersecurity outcomes and activities. These categories and subcategories are aligned with existing standards, guidelines, and practices, allowing organizations to leverage their current cybersecurity initiatives and map them to the framework.

The NIST CSF is designed to be a living document, regularly updated to reflect the evolving cybersecurity landscape and emerging threats. It provides a common language and unified approach for organizations to communicate their cybersecurity posture internally and externally with stakeholders, regulators, and partners.

By adopting the NIST CSF, organizations can better understand and manage their cybersecurity risks, prioritize investments, and foster a culture of cybersecurity awareness and preparedness throughout their operations.

4.2 NIST SP 800-53 SECURITY AND PRIVACY CONTROLS

NIST Special Publication 800-53 is a comprehensive catalogue of security and privacy controls developed by the National Institute of Standards and Technology (NIST). This publication provides a comprehensive set of safeguards and countermeasures to protect federal information systems and organizations from a diverse range of threats, including hostile cyber-attacks, natural disasters, structural failures, and human errors.

The controls outlined in NIST SP 800-53 are designed to be flexible and adaptable, allowing organizations to tailor and implement them based on their specific risk management strategies, mission and business requirements, and organizational priorities. The publication provides a risk-based approach to selecting and implementing security controls, ensuring that organizations can effectively manage their cybersecurity risks while optimizing their resources.

NIST SP 800-53 organizes the security and privacy controls into 20 distinct families, each addressing a specific aspect of information security. These families cover areas such as access control, audit and accountability, configuration management, incident response, risk assessment, system and communications protection, and system and information integrity.

Each control within these families is assigned a baseline level of assurance. low, moderate, or high. These baselines provide a starting point for organizations to select and implement the appropriate controls based on their risk tolerance and the potential impact of a security breach or data loss.

In addition to the security controls, NIST SP 800-53 provides guidance on control selection, implementation, and assessment. It offers a comprehensive approach to continuous monitoring, which involves ongoing assessments and risk management activities to ensure that security controls are effective and remain in compliance with organizational policies and regulatory requirements.

The publication is regularly updated to address evolving threats, technological advancements, and changes in organizational requirements. This ensures that the security and privacy controls remain relevant and effective in protecting critical information systems and data.

By adopting the security and privacy controls outlined in NIST SP 800-53, organizations can establish a comprehensive and risk-based approach to cybersecurity, promoting consistency, efficiency, and effective risk management across their information systems and operations.

4.3 CIS CRITICAL SECURITY CONTROLS

The CIS Critical Security Controls (CIS Controls) are a prioritized set of cyber defense safeguards developed by the Center for Internet Security (CIS) to help organizations protect against the most common and dangerous cyber attacks. These controls provide a pragmatic and effective approach to cybersecurity, focusing on the most critical areas of risk mitigation.

The CIS Controls are based on the principle of "offense informing defense," which means that the controls are continuously updated and refined based on the latest real-world cyber attack data and threat intelligence. This ensures that the controls remain relevant and effective in addressing the evolving threat landscape.

The CIS Controls are organized into three categories. Basic, Foundational, and Organizational. Each category includes a subset of controls that address specific security objectives and defense layers.

The Basic Controls (CIS Controls 1-6) focus on essential cyber hygiene practices, such as inventory and control of hardware assets, software inventory and secure configurations, and continuous vulnerability management.

The Foundational Controls (CIS Controls 7-16) build upon the Basic Controls and address more advanced security concepts, including access control, malware defenses, data protection, incident response, and security awareness training.

The Organizational Controls (CIS Controls 17-20) address the governance and management aspects of cybersecurity, including risk assessment, incident response and management, and penetration testing and red team exercises.

Each CIS Control is accompanied by detailed implementation guidance, including specific actions, tools, and resources to help organizations effectively implement and maintain the control. The CIS Controls also provide metrics and measurement criteria to help organizations assess their security posture and identify areas for improvement.

By adopting the CIS Critical Security Controls, organizations can establish a solid foundation for their cybersecurity program, addressing the most critical areas of risk and aligning their security efforts with industry best practices. The controls are designed to be scalable and adaptable, suitable for organizations of all sizes and across various industries.

Regular reassessment and continuous improvement are essential components of the CIS Controls approach, ensuring that organizations stay ahead of emerging threats and maintain a robust security posture over time.

4.4 MAPPING CONTROLS TO SECURITY REQUIREMENTS

Mapping security controls to an organization's specific requirements is a crucial step in establishing an effective cybersecurity program. It ensures that the implemented controls directly address the unique risks, regulatory obligations, and operational needs of the organization, rather than adopting a one-size-fits-all approach.

The process of mapping controls typically involves the following key steps:

1. **Identify organizational requirements**. This includes understanding the organization's risk appetite, compliance mandates (e.g., PCI DSS, HIPAA, GDPR), industry standards, and business objectives. Gathering input from stakeholders across different departments is essential to capture a comprehensive set of requirements.
2. **Select relevant control frameworks**. Based on the identified requirements, organizations can select appropriate control frameworks and standards to reference. Common frameworks include NIST SP 800-53, ISO 27001, CIS Controls, and sector-specific guidelines.
3. **Analyse control catalogs**. Thoroughly review the controls provided by the selected frameworks, assessing their relevance and applicability to the organization's specific requirements. This may involve mapping controls to specific risks, regulatory obligations, or business processes.
4. **Prioritize and tailor controls**. Based on the analysis, organizations can prioritize the most critical controls and tailor their implementation to align with their unique needs. This may involve adapting control

parameters, defining compensating controls, or providing supplemental guidance.

5. **Develop an implementation plan**. Create a detailed plan that outlines the selected controls, their mapping to organizational requirements, implementation timelines, responsible parties, and resource allocation.

6. **Implement and monitor controls**. Execute the implementation plan, deploying the selected controls across the organization's systems, processes, and operations. Continuously monitor the effectiveness of the implemented controls and adjust as needed.

Effective control mapping requires close collaboration between various stakeholders, including security professionals, risk managers, compliance officers, and business process owners. This cross-functional approach ensures that the implemented controls align with the organization's overall security strategy and operational objectives.

Regular reviews and updates to the control mapping are necessary to address changes in the organization's risk landscape, evolving threats, and emerging regulatory or industry requirements. This iterative process helps maintain a robust and adaptive security posture aligned with the organization's dynamic needs.

4.5 CONTROL IMPLEMENTATION AND ASSESSMENT

Effective control implementation and assessment are critical components of a robust cybersecurity program. They ensure that the selected security controls are properly deployed, configured, and operating as intended to mitigate identified risks and meet organizational requirements.

Control implementation involves a structured approach that typically includes the following steps:

1. **Develop implementation plans**. For each selected control, create detailed implementation plans that outline the specific actions, responsibilities, timelines, and resources required for successful deployment.

2. **Configure and deploy controls**. Based on the implementation plans, configure, and deploy the security controls across the organization's systems, networks, applications, and processes. This may involve technical implementations, policy updates, procedure changes, or a combination of these elements.

3. **Document control implementation**. Maintain comprehensive documentation of the implemented controls, including configurations, settings, and any deviations or compensating controls applied. This documentation serves as a reference for ongoing maintenance and assessment activities.

4. **Communicate and train**. Ensure that all relevant stakeholders, including end-users, system administrators, and security personnel, are properly trained on the implemented controls and their associated procedures.

Assessment is an essential step in evaluating the effectiveness of implemented controls and identifying any gaps or areas for improvement. It typically involves the following activities:

1. **Control testing**. Conduct rigorous testing to verify that the implemented controls are operating as intended and meeting their stated objectives. This may include penetration testing, vulnerability assessments, and compliance audits.
2. **Continuous monitoring**. Implement processes and tools for continuous monitoring of control effectiveness, including log analysis, security information and event management (SIEM), and ongoing vulnerability scanning.
3. **Control evaluation**. Analyse the results of control testing and monitoring activities to assess the overall effectiveness of the implemented controls and identify any control deficiencies or areas for enhancement.
4. **Corrective actions**. Based on the control evaluation, develop, and implement corrective action plans to address identified control deficiencies, update configurations, or introduce new controls as necessary.

Effective control implementation and assessment require close collaboration between security professionals, system administrators, compliance teams, and business stakeholders. Regular communication and clear lines of responsibility are essential for ensuring that controls are properly deployed, maintained, and continuously evaluated for effectiveness.

By adopting a structured approach to control implementation and assessment, organizations can maintain a robust security posture, demonstrate compliance with regulatory requirements, and foster a culture of continuous improvement in their cybersecurity practices.

4.6 WORKSHOP EXERCISE: CYBERSECURITY FRAMEWORKS & CONTROLS

Workshop Exercise - Aligning Security Controls with Business Needs

Scenario: You are a cybersecurity consultant for a small to medium-sized company called "CloudHaven." CloudHaven provides cloud-based document storage and collaboration solutions for businesses. They have recently experienced a data breach that compromised sensitive customer information. In response to this incident, CloudHaven's leadership team has recognized the need to improve their cybersecurity posture. They have hired you to conduct a security assessment and develop a plan for implementing appropriate cybersecurity controls.

Instructions: This workshop can be completed individually or in groups of 2-4 students. Please submit a written report of your findings in the designated

Workshop document downloaded from the Assignments folder (400 words maximum).

Your report should address the following aspects (a paragraph for each point):

1. Identify Business Requirements and Regulatory Landscape:

1. Analyse CloudHaven's business model and identify their critical assets, including data types they store and process.
2. Research relevant industry regulations and compliance requirements that CloudHaven might be subject to, such as data privacy regulations or cloud security standards.

2. Security Risk Assessment:

1. Based on the identified business requirements and regulatory landscape, conduct a high-level security risk assessment for CloudHaven.
2. Consider potential threats, vulnerabilities, and the impact of a security incident on CloudHaven's operations and reputation.

3. Mapping Controls to Requirements:

1. Leveraging your knowledge of cybersecurity frameworks covered in Module 4 (NIST CSF, NIST SP 800-53, CIS Controls), recommend a selection of security controls that address the identified risks and align with CloudHaven's business needs and regulatory requirements.
2. Explain the rationale behind your control selection and how they mitigate specific risks.

Additional Considerations:

- Use relevant security terminology to demonstrate your understanding of the materials covered in Module 4.
- You may use external resources to support your explanations, but ensure all information is properly cited.
- Focus on providing practical recommendations that are tailored to the specific needs of CloudHaven, a small to medium-sized business in the cloud storage industry.

Remember: There are no right or wrong answers here. The goal is to demonstrate your ability to apply your knowledge of cybersecurity frameworks and control selection to a real-world scenario.

By completing this workshop, you will gain valuable insights into:

- Aligning cybersecurity controls with an organization's specific business needs and regulatory requirements.
- Prioritizing security risks and selecting appropriate controls for mitigation.
- Addressing implementation challenges faced by small to medium-sized businesses. Developing a risk-based approach to cybersecurity control implementation.

NOTES

MODULE 5.
IDENTITY & ACCESS MANAGEMENT

Module Summary. This module covers essential concepts and techniques related to identity and access management (IAM). It begins by discussing authentication and authorization mechanisms, which work together to verify user identities and control their access privileges. Key topics include password policies, biometrics, cryptographic authentication, multi-factor authentication (MFA), least privilege principle, role-based access control (RBAC), and privileged access management (PAM).

The module then looks into IAM systems, which provide a centralized platform for managing digital identities, authentication, authorization, and access management tools. It also explores RBAC, a widely adopted model that assigns permissions based on roles rather than individual users, promoting least privilege and simplifying access control administration.

Also highlighted are the PAM practices for securing and monitoring privileged accounts with elevated access rights. Finally, it covers single sign-on (SSO) for seamless access across multiple applications and MFA for enhanced security through additional authentication factors beyond passwords.

5.1 AUTHENTICATION AND AUTHORIZATION MECHANISMS

Authentication and authorization are fundamental security controls that work in tandem to ensure only legitimate users and entities can access systems, applications, and data. These mechanisms form the foundation of an effective identity and access management (IAM) strategy.

Authentication mechanisms verify the identity of a user, device, or system attempting to access resources. Common authentication methods include:

1. **Passwords.** Users provide a secret alphanumeric string known only to them. Strong password policies and multi-factor authentication enhance password security.
2. **Biometrics.** Unique physical or behavioural characteristics like fingerprints, facial recognition, or voice patterns are used to verify an individual's identity.
3. **Cryptographic authentication.** Digital certificates, cryptographic keys, or other cryptographic techniques authenticate the user or system.
4. **Multi-factor authentication (MFA).** Combining two or more authentication factors like a password and a one-time code sent to a registered device.

Once a user or entity is authenticated, authorization mechanisms determine their level of access and permitted actions within a system or application. Authorization is typically based on predefined policies, roles, and rules that govern access privileges.

Key authorization concepts include:

1. **Least privilege.** Users are granted only the minimum access required to perform their job functions, reducing the risk of accidental or malicious actions.
2. **Role-based access control (RBAC).** Permissions are assigned based on an individual's job role within the organization.
3. **Attribute-based access control (ABAC).** Access is granted based on attributes like user location, device posture, or risk levels, providing dynamic and contextual access control.
4. **Privileged access management (PAM).** Elevated privileges for administrative tasks are tightly controlled and monitored to prevent misuse.

Effective authentication and authorization mechanisms are essential for maintaining a secure environment, protecting sensitive data, and ensuring regulatory compliance. They help prevent unauthorized access, limit the potential for data breaches, and support the principle of least privilege.

Regular reviews, updates, and continuous monitoring of these mechanisms are necessary to address evolving threats, changes in user roles, and new regulatory requirements. A robust IAM strategy centred around strong authentication and authorization controls is a cornerstone of any organization's cybersecurity program.

5.2 IDENTITY AND ACCESS MANAGEMENT (IAM) SYSTEMS

Identity and Access Management (IAM) systems are a critical component of an organization's security infrastructure. IAM systems are designed to manage digital identities, authenticate users, and control access to systems and resources. IAM systems provide a centralized platform for managing user access across an organization, ensuring that the right people have access to the right resources at the right time.

IAM systems typically consist of several components, including a user directory, authentication mechanisms, authorization mechanisms, and access management tools. The user directory is a database that stores information about users, including usernames, passwords, and other attributes. Authentication mechanisms are used to verify the identity of users, while authorization mechanisms are used to determine what resources a user is allowed to access. Access management tools are used to manage user access to systems and resources.

One of the primary benefits of IAM systems is that they enable organizations to implement role-based access control (RBAC). RBAC is a method of controlling access to resources based on a user's role within the organization. For example, a user in the role of "employee" may have access to different resources than a user in the role of "manager." RBAC simplifies access management by reducing the number of access control decisions that need to be made.

Another critical component of IAM systems is privileged access management (PAM). PAM is a set of tools and processes designed to manage access to sensitive systems and resources. PAM solutions typically include features such as password vaulting, session monitoring, and access request workflows. PAM solutions enable organizations to control access to sensitive systems and resources, reduce the risk of insider threats, and ensure compliance with regulatory requirements.

Single sign-on (SSO) and multi-factor authentication (MFA) are two other critical components of IAM systems. SSO allows users to log in once and access multiple systems and resources without having to log in again. MFA requires users to provide two or more forms of authentication, such as a password and a fingerprint or a password and a one-time code sent to a mobile device. SSO and MFA improve security by reducing the risk of password-related attacks and increasing user convenience.

IAM systems play a critical role in an organization's security infrastructure. By managing digital identities, authenticating users, and controlling access to systems and resources, IAM systems help organizations ensure that the right people have access to the right resources at the right time. IAM systems enable organizations to implement role-based access control, privileged access management, single sign-on, and multi-factor authentication, all of which improve security and reduce the risk of data breaches. When implementing IAM systems, it is essential to follow best practices, such as regularly reviewing access rights, implementing strong password policies, and providing regular training to users.

5.3 ROLE-BASED ACCESS CONTROL (RBAC)

Role-based access control (RBAC) is a widely adopted access control mechanism that regulates permissions and access to resources based on the roles assigned to individuals or entities within an organization. Unlike traditional access control models that grant permissions directly to users, RBAC introduces the concept of roles, which serve as intermediaries between users and permissions.

In an RBAC system, roles are defined based on job functions, responsibilities, and the level of access required to perform specific tasks within an organization. These roles are then assigned a set of permissions that determine the actions they can perform and the resources they can access. Users are assigned one or more roles based on their responsibilities and duties within the organization.

The primary advantage of RBAC is its ability to simplify the administration and management of access control. Instead of assigning permissions directly to individual users, administrators can focus on defining roles and assigning appropriate permissions to those roles. When a new user joins the organization or an existing user's responsibilities change, the administrator simply needs to assign or modify the user's role, automatically granting or revoking the necessary permissions.

RBAC also promotes the principle of least privilege, which states that users should only be granted the minimum permissions required to perform their job functions. By assigning roles with specific permissions, RBAC ensures that users cannot access resources or perform actions beyond their authorized scope, reducing the risk of unauthorized access and potential security breaches.

Furthermore, RBAC facilitates auditing and compliance by providing a clear mapping between roles and their associated permissions. This transparency allows organizations to easily review and validate the access rights granted to each role, ensuring compliance with regulatory requirements and internal policies.

RBAC can be implemented in various contexts, including operating systems, databases, applications, and cloud environments. Many organizations adopt RBAC as part of their overall security strategy, as it helps to enforce access control policies consistently across different systems and applications, while also simplifying the management of user permissions and access rights.

5.4 PRIVILEGED ACCESS MANAGEMENT (PAM)

Privileged access management (PAM) is a set of practices and technologies designed to manage and control access to privileged accounts and resources within an organization. Privileged accounts, such as system administrator accounts, root accounts, and service accounts, possess elevated permissions and access rights that can potentially cause significant damage if misused or compromised.

The primary goal of PAM is to minimize the risk associated with privileged access by implementing strict controls and monitoring mechanisms. It ensures that privileged access is granted only to authorized individuals, for specific tasks, and for a limited duration, adhering to the principle of least privilege.

PAM typically involves the following key components and practices.

1. **Privileged account discovery**. Identifying and maintaining an inventory of all privileged accounts across the organization's systems and applications.
2. **Credential management**. Securely storing, rotating, and managing privileged account credentials, such as passwords and encryption keys,

using tools like password vaults or privileged access management software.

3. **Access control and approval workflows**. Implementing processes and workflows to govern and approve privileged access requests, ensuring that access is granted only when necessary and for specific purposes.

4. **Session monitoring and recording**. Monitoring and recording all privileged user sessions, allowing for auditing, incident response, and forensic analysis if needed.

5. **Least privilege enforcement**. Granting only the minimum necessary privileges required for a specific task or role, minimizing the potential for unauthorized access or actions.

6. **Privileged access analytics**. Analysing privileged user activities, access patterns, and behaviours to detect and respond to potential threats or policy violations.

By implementing PAM practices and technologies, organizations can better protect their critical systems and data from insider threats, external attacks, and accidental misuse of privileged accounts. PAM also helps organizations comply with regulatory requirements and industry standards related to privileged access management and data protection.

Effective PAM requires a comprehensive approach that combines people, processes, and technology, ensuring that privileged access is tightly controlled, monitored, and audited throughout the entire lifecycle of privileged accounts and activities.

5.5 SINGLE SIGN-ON (SSO) AND MULTI-FACTOR AUTHENTICATION (MFA)

SINGLE SIGN-ON (SSO).

Single sign-on is an authentication mechanism that allows users to access multiple applications or services with a single set of credentials. Rather than having to remember and enter separate usernames and passwords for each application, users can log in once and gain access to all authorized resources without needing to re-authenticate.

SSO works by establishing trust relationships between an identity provider (IdP) and multiple service providers (SPs). The IdP authenticates the user and issues a security token or assertion, which is then used by the SPs to grant access to their respective applications or services.

The primary benefits of SSO include improved user experience, increased productivity, and reduced administrative overhead. Users don't have to remember multiple credentials, and IT teams don't have to manage and reset passwords for various applications.

MULTI-FACTOR AUTHENTICATION (MFA).

Multi-factor authentication is a security mechanism that requires users to provide two or more forms of authentication before granting access to an application, system, or resource. The goal of MFA is to enhance security by adding an extra layer of protection beyond just a username and password.

The three common factors used in MFA are.

1. Something you know (e.g., password, PIN)
2. Something you have (e.g., security token, mobile device)
3. Something you are (e.g., biometric data like fingerprint or facial recognition)

By combining two or more of these factors, MFA significantly reduces the risk of unauthorized access, even if one factor is compromised. For example, a user might need to enter a password (something they know) and provide a one-time code generated by a mobile app or token (something they have).

MFA adds an extra layer of security and is widely recommended for protecting sensitive data, critical systems, and high-risk applications. It helps mitigate the risk of credential theft, phishing attacks, and other forms of unauthorized access.

Both SSO and MFA are essential components of modern identity and access management (IAM) solutions. While SSO improves user experience and productivity, MFA enhances security by requiring additional authentication factors beyond just a password. Organizations often implement both SSO and MFA together to strike a balance between convenience and strong security measures.

5.6 WORKSHOP EXERCISE:
IDENTITY & ACCESS MANAGEMENT (IAM)

Workshop Exercise - Securing User Access with IAM

Scenario: You are a cybersecurity consultant working for a consulting firm. You have been assigned to a new client, "Acme Inc." - a leading manufacturer of industrial robots used in various industries. Acme Inc. is undergoing rapid growth and is increasingly reliant on digital technologies for its operations. They have recently experienced a few security incidents involving unauthorized access to user accounts and sensitive data. These incidents have highlighted the need for a more robust identity and access management (IAM) strategy. Acme Inc.'s management team has requested your expertise in assessing their current IAM practices and developing recommendations for improvement.

Instructions: This workshop can be completed individually or in groups of 2-4 students. Please submit a written report of your findings in the designated Workshop document downloaded from the Assignments folder (400 words maximum).

Your report should address the following aspects (one para per point):

1. Current State Assessment:

1. Conduct a high-level assessment of Acme Inc.'s current IAM practices. This may involve reviewing existing documentation, interviewing relevant personnel, and analyzing user access logs.
2. Identify key areas of strength and weakness in their current approach to authentication, authorization, and access control.

2. Security Requirements and Regulatory Landscape:

1. Analyse Acme Inc.'s business model and identify the types of sensitive data they collect, store, and process.
2. Research relevant industry regulations and compliance requirements that Acme Inc. might be subject to, such as data privacy regulations or industry-specific security standards.

3. IAM Recommendations:

1. Based on the identified security requirements, regulatory landscape, and current state assessment, recommend specific improvements to Acme Inc.'s IAM strategy.
2. Consider factors like strengthening authentication mechanisms (e.g., implementing MFA), implementing role-based access control (RBAC), and leveraging privileged access management (PAM) for high-risk accounts.

Additional Considerations:

- Use relevant security terminology to demonstrate your understanding of the materials covered in Module 5.
- You may use external resources to support your explanations, but ensure all information is properly cited.
- Focus on providing practical recommendations that are tailored to the specific needs of Acme Inc., considering their industry, size, and current security posture.

There are no right or wrong answers here. The goal is to demonstrate your ability to apply your knowledge of IAM concepts and best practices to a real-world scenario.

By completing this workshop, you will gain valuable insights into:

- Conducting a security assessment of an organization's IAM practices.
- Aligning IAM strategies with security requirements and regulatory compliance.
- Selecting appropriate authentication and authorization mechanisms.
- Implementing IAM solutions while considering user adoption and operational impact.

Developing a comprehensive IAM strategy for an organization undergoing growth.

NOTES

MODULE 6.
DATA PROTECTION &PRIVACY

Module 6 examines the critical aspects of data protection and privacy, exploring cryptographic techniques, key management, public key infrastructure (PKI), data privacy regulations like GDPR and the Privacy Act, as well as essential controls and compliance measures to safeguard sensitive information in today's data-driven landscape.

6.1 CRYPTOGRAPHY AND ENCRYPTION TECHNIQUES

Cryptography and encryption techniques play a crucial role in securing data and ensuring confidentiality, integrity, and authenticity during transmission and storage. These techniques involve the use of algorithms and mathematical functions to transform plaintext data into ciphertext, making it unreadable to anyone without the proper decryption keys or mechanisms.

One of the fundamental encryption techniques is symmetric encryption, which uses a single shared secret key for both encryption and decryption processes. Examples of symmetric encryption algorithms include Advanced Encryption Standard (AES), Data Encryption Standard (DES), and Triple DES (3DES). These algorithms are widely used for securing data at rest and in transit, as well as for securing communication channels.

Asymmetric encryption, also known as public-key cryptography, employs a pair of mathematically related keys. a public key for encryption and a private key for decryption. This approach is commonly used in secure communication protocols, digital signatures, and key exchange mechanisms. Popular asymmetric encryption algorithms include RSA, Elliptic Curve Cryptography (ECC), and Diffie-Hellman.

Hashing algorithms, such as SHA-256 and SHA-3, are used to generate unique fixed-length digests or hash values from input data. These algorithms are one-way functions, meaning it is computationally infeasible to reconstruct the original data from the hash value. Hashing is widely used for data integrity checking, password storage, and digital signature generation.

Cryptographic protocols, like Transport Layer Security (TLS) and Secure Sockets Layer (SSL), combine various cryptographic techniques to provide secure communication channels over insecure networks like the internet. These protocols use asymmetric encryption for key exchange, symmetric encryption for bulk data encryption, and hashing for message authentication and integrity verification.

Modern encryption techniques also include advanced concepts like homomorphic encryption, which allows computations to be performed on encrypted data without decrypting it, and quantum-resistant algorithms designed to withstand attacks from powerful quantum computers.

Effective implementation of cryptography and encryption techniques requires careful key management, secure key storage, and proper configuration of encryption algorithms and parameters. Additionally, organizations must comply with relevant regulations and industry standards, such as the Federal Information Processing Standards (FIPS) and the Payment Card Industry Data Security Standard (PCI DSS), which provide guidelines for the use of cryptography in specific contexts.

6.2 KEY MANAGEMENT LIFECYCLE

The key management lifecycle is a comprehensive process that governs the creation, distribution, storage, usage, and eventual destruction of cryptographic keys. Proper key management is essential for maintaining the confidentiality, integrity, and availability of encrypted data and ensuring the overall effectiveness of cryptographic systems.

The key management lifecycle typically consists of the following stages.

1. **Key generation**. This initial stage involves the creation of new cryptographic keys using approved algorithms and parameters. Keys can be generated centrally or distributed across multiple systems, depending on the security requirements.
2. **Key distribution**. After generation, keys must be securely distributed to authorized parties or systems that require them for encryption, decryption, or other cryptographic operations. This distribution process must ensure the keys are not compromised during transit.
3. **Key storage**. Cryptographic keys must be stored securely, either in hardware security modules (HSMs), secure key vaults, or other protected environments. Access to stored keys should be strictly controlled and audited.
4. **Key usage**. Keys are used for various cryptographic operations, such as encryption, decryption, digital signing, and verification. Proper key usage policies and access controls must be in place to prevent unauthorized or improper use of keys.
5. **Key rotation**. For enhanced security, cryptographic keys should be periodically rotated or replaced with new keys. This rotation process helps minimize the risk of key compromise and limits the potential exposure of encrypted data.
6. **Key archival and recovery**. In some cases, keys may need to be archived for future data recovery or compliance purposes. Archived keys must be securely stored and protected, with appropriate access controls and recovery procedures in place.
7. **Key revocation and destruction**. When keys are no longer needed, or if they are suspected of being compromised, they must be revoked and securely destroyed to prevent unauthorized access or misuse.

Throughout the key management lifecycle, processes such as key backup, key escrow (for recovery purposes), and key inventory management may also be involved, depending on the organization's security requirements and compliance needs.

Effective key management is critical for maintaining the integrity and security of cryptographic systems. Organizations typically rely on dedicated key management solutions, such as hardware security modules (HSMs) and key management servers, to automate and streamline the key management lifecycle processes.

6.3 PUBLIC KEY INFRASTRUCTURE (PKI)

A public key infrastructure (PKI) is a system designed to facilitate the secure exchange and verification of digital certificates and public-private key pairs. It provides a framework for managing the creation, distribution, revocation, and renewal of digital certificates, which are used to establish secure communication channels, authenticate parties, and ensure data integrity and non-repudiation.

The main components of a PKI include.

1. **Certificate Authority (CA).** A trusted third-party entity responsible for issuing, managing, and revoking digital certificates. The CA validates the identity of individuals or organizations before issuing certificates and maintains a certificate revocation list (CRL) for revoked certificates.
2. **Registration Authority (RA).** An optional component that acts as an intermediary between the CA and the end entities (users or devices). The RA verifies the identities of end entities and submits certificate requests to the CA.
3. **Digital Certificates**. These are electronic documents that bind a public key to an entity's identity information, such as name, organization, and email address. Certificates are digitally signed by the issuing CA to ensure their authenticity and integrity.
4. **Public and Private Keys**. PKI relies on asymmetric cryptography, where each entity has a pair of mathematically related keys. a public key for encryption and verification, and a private key for decryption and digital signing.

The PKI workflow typically follows these steps.

1. An end entity (user or device) generates a public-private key pair and submits a certificate signing request (CSR) to the Registration Authority or directly to the Certificate Authority.
2. The RA (if present) verifies the end entity's identity and forwards the CSR to the CA.
3. The CA validates the information, generates the digital certificate, signs it with its private key, and issues the certificate to the end entity.

4. The end entity can then use the certificate and its private key for secure communication, authentication, and digital signing purposes.

PKI enables secure communication and transactions over insecure networks like the internet by providing a trusted means of verifying the identities of parties involved and ensuring the integrity and confidentiality of exchanged data. PKI is widely used in various applications, such as secure web browsing (HTTPS), email encryption, code signing, and virtual private networks (VPNs).

Proper PKI implementation and management are critical for maintaining the overall security and trust of the system, including regular certificate renewal, revocation of compromised certificates, and adherence to industry standards and best practices.

6.4 DATA PRIVACY REGULATIONS (GDPR, PRIVACY ACT)

GENERAL DATA PROTECTION REGULATION (GDPR).

The GDPR is a comprehensive data protection regulation enacted by the European Union (EU) in 2018. It aims to protect the personal data and privacy rights of individuals within the EU and the European Economic Area (EEA). The key principles and requirements of the GDPR include.

1. Lawful, fair, and transparent processing of personal data.
2. Purpose limitation, ensuring data is collected for specific, legitimate purposes.
3. Data minimization, limiting data collection to only what is necessary.
4. Accuracy and storage limitation of personal data.
5. Integrity and confidentiality of personal data through appropriate security measures.
6. Accountability and demonstration of compliance by data controllers and processors.
7. Strict rules for obtaining consent for data processing.
8. Enhanced rights for data subjects, including the right to access, rectify, erase, and port their data.
9. Mandatory data breach notification requirements.
10. Strict penalties for non-compliance, with fines up to 4% of a company's global annual revenue.

The GDPR has a broad territorial scope and applies to organizations processing personal data of individuals within the EU, regardless of the organization's location.

PRIVACY ACT.

The Privacy Act is a United States federal law enacted in 1974 to govern the collection, maintenance, use, and dissemination of personal information by federal agencies. The key provisions of the Privacy Act include.

1. Fair Information Practice Principles, which outline requirements for the collection, use, and management of personal data.
2. Restrictions on the disclosure of personal information without the individual's consent.
3. Allowing individuals to access and amend their records held by federal agencies.
4. Establishing rules for maintaining accurate, relevant, and complete records.
5. Requiring agencies to publish notices in the Federal Register describing their systems of records.
6. Establishing procedures for individuals to request access to and amendment of their records.
7. Imposing civil and criminal penalties for non-compliance.

The Privacy Act applies to personal information maintained by federal agencies but does not directly regulate the private sector. However, many state laws and industry-specific regulations incorporate similar privacy principles.

Both the GDPR and the Privacy Act aim to protect individuals' privacy rights and establish rules and guidelines for organizations handling personal data. Compliance with these regulations is crucial for organizations operating within their respective jurisdictions to avoid substantial fines, legal implications, and reputational damage.

6.5 DATA PROTECTION CONTROLS AND COMPLIANCE

Data protection controls are the measures, policies, and practices implemented by organizations to safeguard sensitive and confidential data from unauthorized access, modification, disclosure, or destruction. These controls are essential for maintaining data privacy, integrity, and availability, as well as ensuring compliance with relevant regulations and industry standards.

Some key data protection controls include.

1. **Access controls**. Mechanisms to restrict access to data and systems based on the principle of least privilege, such as user authentication, authorization, and role-based access controls.
2. **Encryption**. The use of cryptographic techniques to protect data at rest (stored data) and data in transit (data being transmitted) from unauthorized access.
3. **Data masking and anonymization**. Techniques to obfuscate or remove personally identifiable information (PII) from data sets, ensuring data privacy while allowing for legitimate data usage.

4. **Data loss prevention (DLP).** Solutions that monitor and control the movement and transfer of sensitive data, preventing unauthorized data exfiltration.

5. **Secure data disposal**. Procedures for securely deleting or destroying data when it is no longer needed, ensuring that sensitive information cannot be recovered or accessed.

6. **Incident response and breach notification**. Processes for detecting, responding to, and reporting data breaches or security incidents involving sensitive data.

7. **Auditing and monitoring**. Mechanisms for logging, monitoring, and auditing access to sensitive data and systems, enabling detection of unauthorized activities and compliance verification.

8. **Security awareness and training**. Programs to educate and train employees on data protection best practices, policies, and their responsibilities in handling sensitive information.

Compliance with data protection regulations and industry standards is crucial for organizations handling sensitive data. Some key regulations and standards include.

1. **General Data Protection Regulation (GDPR).** A comprehensive data protection regulation enacted by the European Union, which outlines strict requirements for handling personal data of EU residents.

2. **Health Insurance Portability and Accountability Act (HIPAA)**. A United States regulation that sets standards for protecting sensitive patient health information.

3. **Payment Card Industry Data Security Standard (PCI DSS)**. A set of security standards for organizations that handle credit card information and other payment data.

4. **ISO/IEC 27001**. An international standard that provides a framework for implementing, maintaining, and continually improving an information security management system (ISMS).

Effective data protection controls and compliance require a holistic approach that combines technical, administrative, and physical safeguards. Organizations must regularly assess their data protection practices, implement appropriate controls, and continuously monitor and update their security measures to address evolving threats and regulatory requirements.

6.6 WORKSHOP EXERCISE: DATA PROTECTION & PRIVACY

Workshop Exercise - Data Protection & Privacy

Scenario: Imagine you are a security consultant tasked with advising a large hospital on fortifying their data security practices. The hospital has recently experienced a data breach where patient information was compromised.

Task: Following the data protection and privacy principles covered in Module 6, develop a comprehensive data security plan to address the hospital's vulnerabilities and prevent future breaches.

Your plan should address the following key areas:

1. Data Classification and Risk Assessment:

1. Identify the different types of sensitive data the hospital stores (e.g., patient medical records, financial information, social security numbers).
2. Classify this data based on its sensitivity level (e.g., high, medium, low) to determine appropriate protection measures.
3. Conduct a risk assessment to identify potential threats and vulnerabilities associated with each data classification.

2. Data Protection Controls:

1. Recommend specific data protection controls based on the risk assessment.
2. Consider controls such as:
   a. **Access Controls**: Implement strong user authentication methods (e.g., multi-factor authentication) and enforce least privilege access principles.
   b. **Encryption**: Encrypt sensitive data at rest and in transit to render it unreadable in case of a breach.
   c. **Data Masking and Anonymization**: Consider anonymizing or masking patient data when possible, for legitimate data analysis purposes.
   d. **Data Loss Prevention (DLP)**: Implement DLP solutions to monitor and prevent unauthorized data exfiltration.

3. Security Awareness and Training:

Briefly mention the need for a security awareness and training program for hospital staff to educate them on data protection best practices, hospital policies, and their role in safeguarding sensitive information.

Deliverables:

A 400-word written report outlining your comprehensive data security plan for the hospital.

The report should be structured with clear headings for each of the addressed areas.

Briefly explain the rationale behind your recommendations and how they address the identified risks and vulnerabilities.

Important Note:

You cannot directly copy and paste content from the internet or learning materials to complete this workshop.

Use the knowledge gained from Module 6 to understand the concepts and then formulate your own data security plan tailored to the hospital scenario.

You can leverage online resources to research specific data protection controls and best practices, but ensure you paraphrase and avoid plagiarism.

This workshop exercise will help you reinforce your understanding of data protection principles, Analyse security risks, and design appropriate control measures to safeguard sensitive information in a healthcare environment.

NOTES

MODULE 7.
NETWORK & APPLICATION SECURITY

Module 7 explores the essential aspects of network and application security, covering network security fundamentals, firewalls, intrusion detection/prevention systems, VPNs, network segmentation, secure protocols, web application security (OWASP Top 10), secure coding practices, and integrating security into the software development lifecycle (SDLC).

7.1 NETWORK SECURITY FUNDAMENTALS

Network security fundamentals are the essential concepts and practices that form the foundation for protecting computer networks and the data transmitted over them from unauthorized access, misuse, and various threats. Understanding these fundamentals is crucial for implementing effective security measures and safeguarding valuable information assets.

One of the primary network security fundamentals is the CIA triad. Confidentiality, Integrity, and Availability. Confidentiality ensures that sensitive information is accessible only to authorized parties, while integrity guarantees that data remains accurate and complete, without unauthorized modifications. Availability ensures that legitimate users can access network resources and services when needed.

Another fundamental principle is the principle of least privilege, which dictates that users and processes should be granted only the minimum permissions and access rights necessary to perform their intended functions. This approach helps minimize the potential impact of security breaches and limits the extent of damage caused by malicious insiders or compromised accounts.

Network segmentation is a critical security measure that involves dividing a larger network into smaller, isolated segments or zones. This approach limits the spread of threats and contains potential breaches within a specific network segment, reducing the overall risk to the entire network infrastructure.

Authentication, authorization, and accounting (AAA) mechanisms are essential for controlling and monitoring access to network resources. Authentication verifies the identity of users or systems, authorization determines their level of access based on defined policies, and accounting logs and tracks activities for auditing and compliance purposes.

Secure protocols, such as Secure Sockets Layer (SSL)/Transport Layer Security (TLS), Internet Protocol Security (IPsec), and Secure Shell (SSH), provide encryption and authentication mechanisms to protect data in transit over insecure networks like the internet.

Vulnerability management processes, including regular patching, software updates, and vulnerability scanning, are crucial for identifying and mitigating known security weaknesses in network devices, operating systems, and applications.

Incident response and disaster recovery plans outline the procedures for detecting, responding to, and recovering from security incidents, such as network breaches, distributed denial-of-service (DDoS) attacks, or system failures, minimizing downtime and data loss.

These network security fundamentals form the basis for implementing various security controls, such as firewalls, intrusion detection/prevention systems (IDS/IPS), virtual private networks (VPNs), and secure wireless technologies. By understanding and applying these fundamental concepts, organizations can develop a robust and comprehensive network security strategy to protect their valuable assets and ensure business continuity.

7.2 FIREWALLS, IDS/IPS, VPNS

FIREWALLS:

A firewall is a security device or software program that monitors and controls incoming and outgoing network traffic based on predetermined security rules. Its primary function is to act as a barrier between trusted and untrusted networks, allowing or blocking traffic based on specified criteria such as source/destination IP addresses, ports, protocols, and application types. Firewalls can be hardware-based (physical appliances) or software-based (running on servers or endpoints).

INTRUSION DETECTION SYSTEMS (IDS) AND INTRUSION PREVENTION SYSTEMS (IPS)

An Intrusion Detection System (IDS) is a security solution that monitors network traffic and system activities for signs of malicious behaviour or policy violations. It analyses data packets, logs, and system events, looking for patterns that match known attack signatures or anomalous activities. When a potential threat is detected, the IDS generates alerts to notify security personnel.

An Intrusion Prevention System (IPS) is an extension of IDS that not only detects threats but also takes immediate action to prevent or mitigate the detected attacks. In addition to monitoring and alerting, an IPS can actively block malicious traffic, terminate connections, reset sessions, or take other preventive measures to stop the attack in progress.

VIRTUAL PRIVATE NETWORKS (VPNS)

A Virtual Private Network (VPN) is a secure communication channel that extends a private network across a public network, such as the internet. VPNs use encryption and authentication mechanisms to create a secure "tunnel" for transmitting data between remote locations or users and a private network.

VPNs provide several security benefits, including.

1. **Confidentiality**. Data transmitted through the VPN tunnel is encrypted, preventing unauthorized access or eavesdropping.
2. **Integrity**. VPNs use hash functions and digital signatures to ensure data integrity and prevent tampering.
3. **Authentication**. VPNs authenticate users and devices before granting access to the private network, preventing unauthorized access.
4. **Access control**. VPNs can enforce access control policies, limiting access to specific resources based on user roles or permissions.

VPNs are widely used to secure remote access to corporate networks, protect sensitive data transmissions, and enable secure communication between branch offices or remote sites over the internet.

Firewalls, IDS/IPS, and VPNs are essential components of a comprehensive network security strategy. Firewalls act as the first line of defence by controlling network traffic, IDS/IPS systems detect and prevent intrusions and attacks, and VPNs provide secure communication channels for remote access and data transmission over untrusted networks.

7.3 NETWORK SEGMENTATION AND SECURE PROTOCOLS

NETWORK SEGMENTATION:

Network segmentation is the practice of dividing a larger network into smaller, isolated segments or zones. This is achieved by using various networking technologies and security controls, such as virtual local area networks (VLANs), firewalls, and access control lists (ACLs). The primary goals of network segmentation are:

1. **Limiting the spread of threats**. By isolating network segments, potential security breaches or malware infections can be contained within a specific zone, preventing lateral movement and minimizing the impact on the entire network.
2. **Separating sensitive resources**. Critical systems, servers, and sensitive data can be isolated on dedicated network segments with strict access controls, reducing the risk of unauthorized access or exposure.
3. **Improving performance and management**. Network segmentation can enhance performance by reducing broadcast traffic and simplifying network management by applying specific policies and configurations to individual segments.

Network segmentation follows various models, such as separating networks by organizational units (e.g., departments), application types (e.g., web servers, databases), or trust levels (e.g., trusted internal networks, untrusted external networks).

SECURE PROTOCOLS:

Secure protocols are communication protocols that incorporate encryption, authentication, and other security mechanisms to protect data in transit and ensure secure communication over untrusted networks, like the internet. Some commonly used secure protocols include:

1. **Secure Sockets Layer (SSL) and Transport Layer Security (TLS).** These cryptographic protocols secure internet communications, such as web browsing, email, and file transfers, by providing encryption, authentication, and data integrity.
2. **Internet Protocol Security (IPsec).** IPsec operates at the network layer and provides end-to-end encryption, authentication, and integrity for Internet Protocol (IP) communications, enabling secure virtual private networks (VPNs) and securing communication between remote sites or devices.
3. **Secure Shell (SSH).** SSH is a cryptographic network protocol that provides secure remote access, file transfers, and remote command execution over unsecured networks. It is widely used for securely administering servers and network devices.
4. **Secure/Multipurpose Internet Mail Extensions (S/MIME).** S/MIME is a standard for secure email communication, enabling digital signatures and encryption of email messages and attachments.
5. **Secure Hypertext Transfer Protocol (HTTPS).** HTTPS is the secure version of the HTTP protocol, using SSL/TLS encryption to secure communication between web browsers and servers, protecting sensitive data like login credentials and financial information.

Secure protocols are essential for maintaining confidentiality, integrity, and authenticity of data transmitted over networks. They are widely used in various applications, such as e-commerce, online banking, remote access solutions, and secure file transfers, to protect against eavesdropping, tampering, and unauthorized access.

7.4 WEB APPLICATION SECURITY (OWASP TOP 10)

Web application security refers to the measures and practices aimed at protecting web applications and their associated data from various security threats and vulnerabilities. Web applications are commonly accessible over the internet, making them potential targets for attacks such as cross-site scripting (XSS), SQL injection, and unauthorized access attempts.

The Open Web Application Security Project (OWASP) is a nonprofit organization dedicated to improving the security of web applications and raising awareness about web application security risks. OWASP maintains a regularly updated list of the top 10 most critical web application security risks, known as the OWASP Top 10.

The OWASP Top 10 for 2021 includes the following vulnerabilities:

1. **Broken Access Control**. Failures in access control mechanisms that allow unauthorized access to sensitive data or functionality.
2. **Cryptographic Failures**. Insecure cryptographic algorithms, improper key management, or inadequate encryption implementation.
3. **Injection**. Untrusted data sent to an interpreter as part of a command or query, leading to potential code injection attacks like SQL injection or command injection.
4. **Insecure Design**. Flaws in the design and architecture of the application that can lead to security vulnerabilities.
5. **Security Misconfiguration**. Insecure default configurations, incomplete or ad hoc deployments, and improper security hardening.
6. **Vulnerable and Outdated Components**. Using outdated or vulnerable components, such as libraries, frameworks, or software modules.
7. **Identification and Authentication Failures**. Improper implementation of authentication and session management mechanisms.
8. **Software and Data Integrity Failures**. Lack of protections against unauthorized modifications to software or data.
9. **Security Logging and Monitoring Failures**. Inadequate logging and monitoring of security-related events, making it difficult to detect and respond to attacks.
10. **Server-Side Request Forgery (SSRF).** Vulnerabilities that allow an attacker to read or update internal resources by causing the server to make requests to unexpected URLs.

The OWASP Top 10 serves as a valuable resource for developers, security professionals, and organizations to understand and prioritize the most prevalent web application security risks. By addressing these vulnerabilities through secure coding practices, regular security testing, and implementing appropriate countermeasures, organizations can significantly reduce the risk of successful attacks on their web applications and protect sensitive data and functionality.

7.5 SECURE CODING PRACTICES AND SDLC SECURITY

Here's an explanation of secure coding practices and integrating security into the software development life cycle (SDLC):

SECURE CODING PRACTICES

Secure coding practices refer to the techniques, guidelines, and best practices followed by developers to write secure and resilient code that is resistant to various security vulnerabilities and threats. These practices aim to minimize the introduction of security flaws during the coding phase and reduce the attack surface of the software. Some key secure coding practices include:

1. **Input Validation**. Properly validating and sanitizing all user input to prevent injection attacks, such as SQL injection, cross-site scripting (XSS), and command injection.
2. **Secure Authentication and Authorization**. Implementing robust authentication and authorization mechanisms, using secure password storage, and following the principle of least privilege.
3. **Secure Handling of Sensitive Data**. Encrypting sensitive data at rest and in transit, securely storing and managing cryptographic keys, and implementing data protection controls.
4. **Secure Communication**. Using secure protocols (e.g., HTTPS, TLS, SSH) for data transmission and implementing secure channel establishment and session management.
5. **Error Handling and Logging**. Properly handling errors and exceptions, avoiding information leakage through error messages, and implementing secure logging practices.
6. **Secure Configuration and Deployment**. Following secure configuration guidelines, disabling unnecessary features, and implementing secure deployment practices.
7. **Regular Code Reviews and Security Testing**. Conducting regular code reviews, static code analysis, and security testing (e.g., penetration testing, fuzzing) to identify and address security vulnerabilities.

SDLC SECURITY

Integrating security into the Software Development Life Cycle (SDLC) is crucial for building secure and resilient software systems. The SDLC encompasses the various phases of software development, from requirements gathering and design to implementation, testing, deployment, and maintenance. Incorporating security considerations throughout the SDLC helps identify and mitigate security risks early, reducing the overall cost and effort required to address security issues later in the development process.

Some key practices for integrating security into the SDLC include:

1. **Security Requirements and Threat Modelling**. Defining security requirements and conducting threat modelling during the planning and design phases to identify potential threats and vulnerabilities.
2. **Secure Design and Architecture**. Incorporating security principles and best practices into the software design and architecture, such as the principle of least privilege, defence in depth, and secure default configurations.
3. **Secure Coding Practices**. Implementing secure coding practices during the implementation phase, as mentioned earlier, to minimize the introduction of security vulnerabilities.
4. **Security Testing**. Performing various security testing activities, such as static code analysis, dynamic application security testing (DAST), and

penetration testing, throughout the development process to identify and remediate security issues.

5. **Secure Deployment and Configuration**. Following secure deployment and configuration practices, including secure infrastructure setup, hardening, and secure deployment processes.
6. **Continuous Monitoring and Maintenance**. Continuously monitoring the software for security vulnerabilities, applying security patches and updates, and implementing secure maintenance practices.

By integrating security into the SDLC, organizations can proactively address security concerns, reduce the risk of security breaches, and improve the overall security posture of their software products and systems. This approach aligns with the principle of "Security by Design," where security is considered an essential aspect throughout the entire software development process, rather than an afterthought.

7.6 WORKSHOP EXERCISE: NETWORK & APPLICATION SECURITY

Workshop Exercise - Network & Application Security

Scenario: Imagine you are a security consultant tasked with assessing the security posture of a fictional company called "Acme Inc." Acme Inc. is a medium-sized e-commerce company that sells sporting goods online. They have a typical client-server architecture with a web application for customers to browse and purchase products.

Your assignment is to develop a comprehensive security plan for Acme Inc. focusing on network and application security.

Instructions: This workshop can be completed individually or in groups of 2-4 students. Please submit a written report of your findings in the designated Workshop document (400 words maximum).

Your report should address the following aspects:

1. Network Security Analysis:

1. Identify the key network security considerations for Acme Inc. based on the CIA triad (Confidentiality, Integrity, Availability).
2. Explain how network segmentation can be implemented to improve Acme Inc.'s security posture.

2. Web Application Security:

1. Identify potential vulnerabilities in Acme Inc.'s web application based on the OWASP Top 10 list. Explain the security risks associated with each vulnerability. (Avoid directly listing all 10 vulnerabilities from the OWASP Top 10. Instead, focus on 2-4 that are most relevant to e-commerce applications)

2. Describe secure coding practices that can be implemented by Acme Inc.'s developers to mitigate the identified vulnerabilities.

3. SDLC Security Integration:

1. Explain the importance of integrating security throughout the Software Development Lifecycle (SDLC) for Acme Inc.'s web application.
2. Outline 3 key security practices that can be implemented at different stages of the SDLC (e.g., requirements gathering, design, testing).

Use relevant security terminology to demonstrate your understanding of the concepts covered in Module 7.

You may use external resources to support your explanations, but ensure all information is properly cited.

Focus on providing practical recommendations that can be implemented by Acme Inc. to improve their network and application security.

Remember: There are no right or wrong answers here. The goal is to demonstrate your understanding of the key principles and your ability to apply them to a realistic scenario.

By completing this workshop, you will gain valuable insights into:

- Implementing a layered security approach for network and application protection.
- Identifying and mitigating common web application vulnerabilities.

Integrating security considerations throughout the software development process.

NOTES

MODULE 8.
SECURITY OPERATIONS & INCIDENT RESPONSE

This module explores security operations and incident response. It covers SOC fundamentals, SIEM systems, incident response planning and execution, digital forensics and evidence handling, and continuous monitoring and threat detection. Learning these topics will equip you with essential skills for proactively safeguarding systems and effectively responding to security incidents.

8.1 SECURITY OPERATIONS CENTRE (SOC) FUNDAMENTALS

A Security Operations Centre (SOC) is a centralized unit responsible for continuous monitoring, analysis, and response to cybersecurity incidents within an organization. It serves as the focal point for all security-related activities, ensuring the protection of an organization's assets and data. SOC fundamentals encompass the essential components and best practices that enable effective security operations.

At the core of a SOC lies a team of highly skilled security analysts and professionals who leverage advanced tools and technologies to detect, analyse, and respond to potential threats. These individuals possess expertise in various domains, including intrusion detection, incident response, digital forensics, and threat intelligence.

One of the primary functions of a SOC is to collect and analyse security-related data from multiple sources, such as firewalls, intrusion detection/prevention systems (IDS/IPS), endpoint protection solutions, and log management systems. This data is then correlated and analysed using security information and event management (SIEM) tools, which provide a centralized platform for aggregating and correlating security events.

The SOC plays a critical role in threat detection and incident response. Security analysts continuously monitor the organization's networks, systems, and applications for any suspicious activities or potential threats. When an incident is detected, the SOC initiates a predefined incident response process, which includes containment, eradication, recovery, and post-incident analysis.

Effective communication and collaboration are essential components of SOC fundamentals. The SOC serves as a hub for sharing threat intelligence, best practices, and incident response strategies across the organization. It coordinates with various stakeholders, including IT operations, risk management, legal, and executive teams, to ensure a cohesive and comprehensive approach to cybersecurity.

Moreover, SOC fundamentals emphasize the importance of continuous improvement and adaptation. Regular security assessments, vulnerability management, and threat intelligence updates are crucial to maintain an effective security posture. The SOC must stay abreast of the latest threats, vulnerabilities, and attack vectors to proactively enhance the organization's security measures.

By implementing SOC fundamentals, organizations can establish a robust cybersecurity framework, enabling them to detect and respond to threats promptly, mitigate risks, and ensure the confidentiality, integrity, and availability of their critical assets and data.

8.2 SECURITY INFORMATION AND EVENT MANAGEMENT (SIEM)

Security information and event management (SIEM) is a crucial component of an effective security operations centre (SOC). SIEM solutions are designed to collect, analyse, and correlate security-related data from various sources within an organization's IT infrastructure. These sources include network devices, servers, applications, endpoints, and security tools such as firewalls, intrusion detection/prevention systems (IDS/IPS), and antivirus software.

The primary function of a SIEM system is to aggregate and centralize security event data, providing a comprehensive view of an organization's security posture. By normalizing and correlating data from disparate sources, SIEM tools can identify patterns, anomalies, and potential threats that might otherwise go unnoticed.

SIEM solutions employ advanced analytics, including rule-based correlation, statistical analysis, and machine learning algorithms, to detect and prioritize security incidents. These capabilities enable security analysts to quickly identify and respond to critical events, reducing the time required to investigate and mitigate threats.

One of the key benefits of SIEM is its ability to provide real-time monitoring and alerting. Security analysts can configure the SIEM system to generate alerts based on predefined rules or anomalous behaviour patterns. These alerts can be escalated to the appropriate personnel or trigger automated response actions, enabling rapid incident response.

SIEM tools also play a crucial role in compliance and reporting. By collecting and storing security event data, organizations can demonstrate compliance with various industry regulations and standards, such as PCI DSS, HIPAA, and GDPR. SIEM systems can generate comprehensive reports and dashboards, providing visibility into an organization's security posture and facilitating auditing and reporting processes.

Effective SIEM implementation and management require careful planning, including defining data sources, configuring log collection, and parsing rules, and establishing correlation rules and alerting thresholds. Additionally, SIEM solutions often integrate with other security tools and platforms, such as security orchestration, automation, and response (SOAR) solutions, to streamline incident response and remediation efforts.

In summary, SIEM solutions are essential components of a robust security operations centre, enabling organizations to centralize security event data, detect and respond to threats in a timely manner, and maintain compliance with regulatory requirements.

8.3 INCIDENT RESPONSE PLANNING AND EXECUTION

Incident response planning and execution are critical components of an effective cybersecurity strategy. An incident response plan outlines the processes, procedures, and actions that an organization will take to detect, respond to, and recover from security incidents, such as cyberattacks, data breaches, or system failures.

Incident response planning involves several key steps:

1. **Establishing an incident response team**. This cross-functional team typically includes IT security professionals, legal and compliance experts, public relations personnel, and representatives from relevant business units. Clear roles and responsibilities should be defined for each team member.
2. **Identifying potential incidents**. Organizations should analyse their assets, vulnerabilities, and potential threats to identify the types of incidents they may face, such as malware infections, distributed denial-of-service (DDoS) attacks, or unauthorized data access.
3. **Developing incident response procedures**. These procedures should outline the steps to be taken during each phase of the incident response process, including preparation, identification, containment, eradication, recovery, and post-incident activities.
4. **Defining communication protocols**. Clear communication channels and protocols should be established to ensure effective coordination and information sharing among the incident response team, stakeholders, and external parties (e.g., law enforcement, regulatory bodies).
5. **Conducting regular training and testing**. Incident response plans should be regularly reviewed, updated, and tested through tabletop exercises or simulations to ensure their effectiveness and identify areas for improvement.

Incident response execution involves implementing the predefined procedures when a security incident occurs. Key steps in this process include:

1. **Incident detection and analysis**. Security monitoring tools and processes are used to detect and analyse potential security incidents, assessing their scope, impact, and severity.

2. **Containment and mitigation**. Immediate actions are taken to limit the spread of the incident and mitigate its impact, such as isolating affected systems, changing credentials, or implementing temporary workarounds.
3. **Eradication and recovery**. Once contained, the root cause of the incident is identified and eliminated, and affected systems are restored to a secure and operational state.
4. **Post-incident activities**. These include conducting a thorough analysis of the incident, documenting lessons learned, updating incident response plans and security measures, and communicating with relevant stakeholders and authorities as necessary.

Effective incident response planning and execution are essential for minimizing the impact of security incidents, protecting an organization's assets and reputation, and ensuring business continuity. Regular review and improvement of incident response processes are crucial in keeping pace with evolving threats and maintaining a robust cybersecurity posture.

8.4 DIGITAL FORENSICS AND EVIDENCE HANDLING

Digital forensics and evidence handling are critical aspects of cybersecurity incident response and investigation. Digital forensics involves the systematic acquisition, preservation, analysis, and interpretation of digital evidence from various sources, such as computers, mobile devices, network traffic, and cloud resources.

The process of digital forensics typically follows a structured approach:

1. **Evidence acquisition**. This involves securely collecting and preserving digital evidence without altering or compromising its integrity. Proper procedures, such as creating forensic images or capturing network traffic, are employed to ensure the admissibility of evidence in legal proceedings.
2. **Evidence preservation**. Digital evidence is highly volatile and can be easily modified or deleted. Proper preservation techniques, such as write-blocking and chain of custody documentation, are essential to maintain the integrity and authenticity of the evidence.
3. **Evidence analysis**. Forensic analysts use specialized tools and techniques to examine the collected evidence, including file system analysis, memory analysis, malware analysis, and data carving. The goal is to uncover relevant information, identify indicators of compromise (IoCs), and reconstruct the events surrounding the incident.
4. **Evidence interpretation**. The findings from the analysis phase are interpreted and documented in a comprehensive report, providing a timeline of events, attribution information, and recommendations for remediation and prevention.

Effective evidence handling is crucial throughout the digital forensics process. Chain of custody procedures ensure that the evidence is properly documented, transported, and stored, maintaining its integrity and admissibility in legal proceedings. Additionally, strict adherence to legal and regulatory requirements, such as search warrants and privacy laws, is essential when handling digital evidence.

Digital forensics and evidence handling play a vital role in various cybersecurity scenarios, including:

1. **Incident response**. Digital forensics aids in identifying the root cause of security incidents, understanding the scope of the compromise, and gathering evidence for legal or disciplinary actions.
2. **Data breach investigations**. Forensic analysis can uncover the extent of a data breach, identify the compromised systems and data, and provide insights into the attacker's methods and motives.
3. **Intellectual property theft**. Digital forensics can help organizations detect and investigate cases of intellectual property theft, trade secret misappropriation, or unauthorized data exfiltration.
4. **Regulatory compliance**. Many industries and regulations, such as the Payment Card Industry Data Security Standard (PCI DSS) and the General Data Protection Regulation (GDPR), require organizations to have incident response and forensic capabilities in place.

By incorporating digital forensics and evidence handling best practices, organizations can enhance their ability to detect, investigate, and respond to cybersecurity incidents, while ensuring the admissibility and integrity of digital evidence for legal proceedings or internal disciplinary actions.

8.5 CONTINUOUS MONITORING AND THREAT DETECTION

Continuous monitoring and threat detection are essential components of an effective cybersecurity strategy. In today's ever-evolving threat landscape, organizations must proactively monitor their IT infrastructure and continuously assess their security posture to identify and respond to potential threats promptly.

Continuous monitoring involves the ongoing collection, analysis, and evaluation of security-related data from various sources within an organization's network, systems, and applications. This data includes logs, network traffic, user activities, system configurations, and other relevant information. The primary goal of continuous monitoring is to identify deviations from established security baselines, detect anomalous behaviour, and uncover potential security incidents or vulnerabilities.

Several techniques and tools are employed for continuous monitoring and threat detection:

1. **Security information and event management (SIEM) systems.** SIEM solutions collect and correlate security event data from multiple sources, enabling real-time monitoring, analysis, and alerting on potential threats.
2. **Intrusion detection and prevention systems (IDS/IPS).** These systems monitor network traffic and system activities, detecting and preventing known and emerging threats based on predefined rules and signatures.
3. **Vulnerability scanning and management.** Regular vulnerability assessments help identify and prioritize vulnerabilities in systems, applications, and network devices, enabling organizations to address them promptly.
4. **Endpoint detection and response (EDR) tools.** EDR solutions continuously monitor and collect data from endpoints, such as workstations and servers, to detect and respond to advanced threats, including malware and insider threats.
5. **User and entity behaviour analytics (UEBA).** UEBA technologies leverage machine learning and behavioural analysis to detect anomalous user activities, indicating potential insider threats or compromised accounts.
6. **Threat intelligence feeds.** Organizations can integrate external threat intelligence sources, which provide up-to-date information on emerging threats, indicators of compromise (IoCs), and best practices for threat detection and mitigation.

Continuous monitoring and threat detection are crucial for several reasons:

1. **Early threat detection.** By continuously monitoring the environment, organizations can detect potential threats at the earliest stages, enabling rapid response and minimizing the impact of security incidents.
2. **Proactive risk management.** Continuous monitoring provides visibility into an organization's security posture, allowing for proactive risk assessment and mitigation strategies.
3. **Compliance and regulatory requirements.** Many industry regulations and standards, such as PCI DSS, HIPAA, and NIST, mandate continuous monitoring and threat detection as part of an organization's security controls.
4. **Incident response and forensics.** Monitoring data and threat intelligence can aid in incident response efforts, providing valuable information for investigation, root cause analysis, and evidence collection.

Effective continuous monitoring and threat detection require a combination of people, processes, and technology. Organizations must establish robust monitoring processes, deploy appropriate security tools and technologies, and maintain a skilled cybersecurity team to analyse and respond to detected threats effectively.

8.6 WORKSHOP EXERCISE:
SECURITY OPERATIONS & INCIDENT RESPONSE

Workshop Exercise - Security Operations & Incident Response

Scenario: Imagine you are a security consultant tasked with assessing the security posture of a fictional company called "Acme Inc." Acme Inc. is a medium-sized healthcare provider with a network of clinics and a central database that stores patient information. Security is paramount for Acme Inc., as any data breach could have severe consequences.

Your assignment is to develop a comprehensive security operations plan for Acme Inc. focusing on security operations, incident response, and continuous threat detection.

Instructions: This workshop can be completed individually or in groups of 2-4 students. Please submit a written report of your findings in the designated Workshop document (400 words maximum).

Your report should address the following aspects:

1. Security Operations Center (SOC) Implementation:

1. Explain the benefits of establishing a Security Operations Center (SOC) for Acme Inc.
2. Considering the nature of Acme Inc.'s business (healthcare), recommend what type of SOC model (in-house, outsourced, or hybrid) would be most suitable and why.

2. Incident Response Planning and Execution:

1. Outline the key phases of an incident response plan and how they would be applied in the context of a ransomware attack on Acme Inc.'s patient database.
2. Explain the importance of evidence handling during incident response and how it can impact legal proceedings.

3. Continuous Monitoring and Threat Detection:

1. Discuss various techniques and tools that can be employed for continuous monitoring and threat detection within Acme Inc.'s IT infrastructure.
2. Explain how threat intelligence can be leveraged to enhance Acme Inc.'s threat detection capabilities.

Additional Considerations:

- Use relevant security terminology to demonstrate your understanding of the concepts covered in Module 8.
- You may use external resources to support your explanations, but ensure all information is properly cited.

- Focus on providing practical recommendations that can be implemented by Acme Inc. to improve their security operations, incident response, and threat detection posture.
- Remember: There are no right or wrong answers here. The goal is to demonstrate your understanding of the key principles and your ability to apply them to a realistic scenario.

By completing this workshop, you will gain valuable insights into:

- The essential role of a Security Operations Centre (SOC) in safeguarding critical systems and data.
- Developing a comprehensive incident response plan to effectively respond to security breaches.

Implementing continuous monitoring and threat detection strategies to proactively identify and mitigate cyber threats.

NOTES

MODULE 9.
SECTOR-SPECIFIC SECURITY STANDARDS

Module 9 explores sector-specific security standards, ensuring robust protection across industries. Delve into Critical Infrastructure Security Standards, Healthcare Security Standards, Defence and Government Security Standards, Payment Card Industry Data Security Standard, and the emerging Zero Trust Security framework, aligning your organization with industry best practices and regulatory compliance.

9.1 CRITICAL INFRASTRUCTURE SECURITY STANDARDS (NERC CIP, SOCI, AESCSF)

Critical infrastructure, such as energy, water, transportation, and telecommunications systems, is vital to the functioning of modern society. Disruptions or cyber-attacks targeting these systems can have severe consequences, impacting public safety, economic stability, and national security. To address these risks, various security standards and frameworks have been developed to enhance the cybersecurity posture of critical infrastructure organizations.

The North American Electric Reliability Corporation (NERC) Critical Infrastructure Protection (CIP) standards are a set of cybersecurity requirements designed specifically for the electric utility industry. These standards cover a wide range of areas, including physical and cyber security, incident response, and recovery planning. The NERC CIP standards are mandatory for all entities operating in the bulk electric system in North America, ensuring a consistent and robust approach to securing this vital infrastructure.

The Singapore Operational Technology (OT) Cybersecurity Code of Practice (SOCI) is a comprehensive framework developed by the Cyber Security Agency of Singapore. It provides guidance and best practices for securing operational technology systems, which are commonly found in critical infrastructure sectors such as energy, utilities, and manufacturing. The SOCI covers areas like risk management, asset management, access control, and incident response, tailored to the unique challenges of OT environments.

The Australian Energy Sector Cyber Security Framework (AESCSF) is a risk-based framework developed by the Australian government to enhance the cybersecurity posture of the country's energy sector. It provides a structured approach to identifying, assessing, and mitigating cyber risks, considering the specific operational and regulatory requirements of the energy industry. The AESCSF promotes a consistent and coordinated approach to cybersecurity across the sector, fostering collaboration and information sharing among stakeholders.

Compliance with these critical infrastructure security standards is essential for organizations operating in these sectors. It not only helps protect against cyber threats but also demonstrates a commitment to ensuring the resilience and continuity of essential services. Implementation of these standards often involves implementing robust access controls, network segmentation, incident response plans, and regular risk assessments.

Furthermore, many of these standards emphasize the importance of collaboration and information sharing among industry partners and government agencies. This cooperative approach enables the timely exchange of threat intelligence, best practices, and mitigation strategies, strengthening the overall security posture of critical infrastructure.

By adhering to these sector-specific security standards, critical infrastructure organizations can enhance their cyber resilience, protect against disruptions, and maintain the trust and confidence of stakeholders and the public they serve.

9.2 HEALTHCARE SECURITY STANDARDS (FISMA, HIPAA)

Healthcare Security Standards (FISMA, HIPAA)

The healthcare industry handles sensitive patient information, making it a prime target for cyber threats. To protect the confidentiality, integrity, and availability of this critical data, various security standards and regulations have been established, including the Federal Information Security Management Act (FISMA) and the Health Insurance Portability and Accountability Act (HIPAA).

FISMA is a United States federal law that defines a comprehensive framework for ensuring the effectiveness of information security controls over information resources that support federal operations and assets. While FISMA primarily applies to federal agencies, its requirements and guidelines are often adopted by healthcare organizations that work with government agencies or handle federal data.

FISMA mandates the development and implementation of information security programs, including risk assessments, security controls, continuous monitoring, and incident response procedures. It also requires independent audits and evaluations to ensure compliance and identify areas for improvement. By adhering to FISMA, healthcare organizations can enhance the security of their information systems and protect sensitive data from unauthorized access, use, disclosure, disruption, modification, or destruction.

HIPAA is a federal law that establishes national standards for the protection of individuals' medical records and other personal health information (PHI). The HIPAA Security Rule specifically outlines administrative, physical, and technical safeguards that covered entities (healthcare providers, health plans, and healthcare clearinghouses) and their business associates must implement to ensure the confidentiality, integrity, and availability of electronic protected health information (ePHI).

The HIPAA Security Rule requires covered entities to conduct risk assessments, implement access controls, encrypt data at rest and in transit, audit system activity, and establish incident response and breach notification procedures. It also mandates the designation of a security official responsible for developing and implementing policies and procedures to safeguard ePHI.

Compliance with HIPAA is not only a legal obligation but also essential for maintaining patient trust and avoiding significant financial penalties and reputational damage resulting from data breaches or non-compliance.

Both FISMA and HIPAA share common goals of protecting sensitive information and ensuring the confidentiality, integrity, and availability of critical data within the healthcare sector. By implementing the security controls and best practices outlined in these standards, healthcare organizations can mitigate risks, detect and respond to security incidents, and ultimately provide better protection for patient data and infrastructure.

9.3 DEFENCE AND GOVERNMENT SECURITY STANDARDS (ASD ESSENTIAL 8, ASD ISM, NIST SP 800-171)

Defence and Government Security Standards (ASD Essential 8, ASD ISM, NIST SP 800-171)

The defence and government sectors handle sensitive and classified information, making robust security standards and practices essential to protect national interests and safeguard critical data. Several security standards have been developed specifically for these sectors, including the Australian Signals Directorate (ASD) Essential Eight, the ASD Information Security Manual (ISM), and the National Institute of Standards and Technology (NIST) Special Publication 800-171.

The ASD Essential Eight is a prioritized list of mitigation strategies developed by the Australian Cyber Security Centre (ACSC) to protect organizations from various cyber threats. These strategies cover areas such as application whitelisting, patching applications, restricting administrative privileges, and implementing multi-factor authentication. By implementing the Essential Eight, organizations can mitigate a significant portion of cyber threats and establish a solid foundation for their cybersecurity posture.

The ASD Information Security Manual (ISM) is a comprehensive cybersecurity framework developed by the Australian Signals Directorate. It provides detailed guidance on implementing effective cybersecurity measures to protect sensitive and classified government information. The ISM covers a wide range of topics, including personnel security, physical security, information technology security, and operational security. It outlines specific controls and best practices tailored to the unique requirements of the Australian government and defence sectors.

The NIST Special Publication 800-171 is a set of security requirements developed by the National Institute of Standards and Technology (NIST) for protecting controlled unclassified information (CUI) in non-federal systems and organizations. It is specifically designed for contractors, subcontractors, and other entities that process, store, or transmit CUI on behalf of federal agencies.

NIST SP 800-171 provides a comprehensive set of security controls spanning areas such as access control, awareness and training, audit and accountability, risk assessment, and system and communications protection. It serves as a baseline for safeguarding sensitive government information and ensuring compliance with federal regulations and contractual requirements.

Compliance with these defence and government security standards is crucial for organizations operating in these sectors or handling sensitive government data. Adherence to these standards not only helps protect critical information assets but also demonstrates a commitment to meeting stringent security requirements and maintaining the trust of government agencies and partners.

Effective implementation of these standards often involves establishing robust governance frameworks, implementing technical controls, conducting regular risk assessments, and providing security awareness training to personnel. Additionally, continuous monitoring and periodic audits are essential to ensure ongoing compliance and identify potential vulnerabilities or areas for improvement.

By adopting these defence and government security standards, organizations can enhance their cybersecurity posture, mitigate risks, and protect sensitive information assets, ultimately contributing to national security and safeguarding critical interests.

9.4 PAYMENT CARD INDUSTRY DATA SECURITY STANDARD (PCI DSS)

The Payment Card Industry Data Security Standard (PCI DSS) is a set of security requirements designed to ensure the protection of cardholder data and prevent credit card fraud. It is a mandatory standard for all organizations that process, store, or transmit payment card information, including merchants, service providers, and financial institutions.

PCI DSS was developed by the Payment Card Industry Security Standards Council (PCI SSC), which comprises major payment card brands such as Visa, Mastercard, American Express, Discover, and JCB. The standard consists of 12 main requirements organized into six control objectives:

1. Build and Maintain a Secure Network and Systems
2. Protect Cardholder Data
3. Maintain a Vulnerability Management Program
4. Implement Strong Access Control Measures

5. Regularly Monitor and Test Networks
6. Maintain an Information Security Policy

These requirements cover a wide range of security controls, including firewalls, encryption, access controls, vulnerability management, monitoring and logging, and regular security testing. PCI DSS also emphasizes the importance of maintaining an information security policy, assigning responsibility for cardholder data protection, and conducting regular risk assessments.

Compliance with PCI DSS is mandatory for any organization that handles payment card data, regardless of its size or industry. Failure to comply can result in significant fines, increased transaction fees, and potential termination of the ability to process credit card payments.

To achieve and maintain PCI DSS compliance, organizations must undergo regular assessments and audits conducted by Qualified Security Assessors (QSAs) or Internal Security Assessors (ISAs). These assessments evaluate the organization's adherence to the PCI DSS requirements and identify any gaps or vulnerabilities that need to be addressed.

In addition to the core requirements, PCI DSS provides supplemental guidance and best practices for specific technologies and environments, such as wireless networks, cloud computing, and point-of-sale (POS) systems.

Compliance with PCI DSS is an ongoing process that requires continuous monitoring, periodic re-evaluation, and adaptation to emerging threats and changes in the payment card industry. By adhering to PCI DSS, organizations can demonstrate their commitment to protecting sensitive cardholder data, maintain the trust of customers and payment card brands, and mitigate the risk of data breaches and associated financial and reputational damages.

9.5 ZERO TRUST SECURITY (EXECUTIVE ORDER 14028)

Zero Trust Security (Executive Order 14028). Zero Trust is a cybersecurity paradigm that operates on the principle of "never trust, always verify." It replaces the traditional perimeter-based security model, which assumes that everything within the network boundary is trusted and everything outside is untrusted. Instead, Zero Trust treats all users, devices, and resources as potential threats and enforces strict access controls and continuous verification.

The Zero Trust security model gained significant attention with the release of Executive Order 14028 by the United States government in May 2021. This executive order aimed to enhance the nation's cybersecurity posture and ensure the secure delivery of critical services. It mandated the adoption of Zero Trust architecture across federal agencies and set guidelines for its implementation.

Key principles of Zero Trust Security outlined in Executive Order 14028 include:

1. **Least Privileged Access**. Users and devices are granted only the minimum necessary access required to perform their tasks, minimizing the potential impact of a compromise.
2. **Micro-segmentation**. Networks and environments are divided into smaller, isolated segments, limiting lateral movement, and containing potential breaches.
3. **Multi-Factor Authentication**. Access to resources requires multiple forms of authentication, such as passwords, biometrics, or hardware tokens, providing an additional layer of security.
4. **Encryption**. Data is encrypted at rest and in transit, protecting it from unauthorized access or interception.
5. **Continuous Monitoring and Validation**. User and device identities, behaviours, and access privileges are continuously monitored and validated, enabling real-time detection of anomalies and potential threats.
6. **Automated Security Enforcement**. Security policies and controls are consistently and automatically enforced across the entire technology stack, reducing the risk of human error or oversight.

The implementation of Zero Trust Security involves a comprehensive overhaul of traditional security architectures, processes, and technologies. It often requires the adoption of modern security solutions like software-defined perimeters, identity and access management systems, next-generation firewalls, and advanced analytics and automation tools.

While Executive Order 14028 primarily focuses on federal agencies, the principles of Zero Trust Security are increasingly being adopted by organizations across various sectors, including healthcare, finance, and critical infrastructure. The zero-trust model offers a more robust and resilient approach to cybersecurity, minimizing the risk of data breaches, insider threats, and cyber-attacks.

As cyber threats continue to evolve, the Zero Trust Security paradigm provides a proactive and comprehensive framework for protecting sensitive data, systems, and resources, ensuring the confidentiality, integrity, and availability of critical assets in today's increasingly complex digital landscape.

9.6 WORKSHOP EXERCISE: SECTOR-SPECIFIC SECURITY STANDARDS

Workshop Exercise - Sector-Specific Security Standards

Scenario: Imagine you are a cybersecurity professional working for a consulting firm. Your firm has been hired by "Acme Inc.", a leading manufacturer of industrial robots used in various industries. Acme Inc. is experiencing significant growth and is expanding its operations globally. They are aware of the increasing importance of cybersecurity and have requested your expertise in identifying relevant security standards and implementing best practices.

Instructions: This workshop can be completed individually or in groups of 2-4 students. Please submit a written report of your findings in the designated Workshop document downloaded from the Assignments folder (400 words maximum).

Your report should address the following aspects:

1. Identify Relevant Security Standards:

Considering the nature of Acme Inc.'s business (industrial robot manufacturing), research and identify at least TWO relevant sector-specific security standards that Acme Inc. should consider implementing. Briefly explain the focus and key requirements of each standard.

2. Risk Assessment and Control Selection:

Conduct a high-level risk assessment for Acme Inc., focusing on potential security threats and vulnerabilities relevant to their industry.

Based on your identified security standards and the risk assessment, recommend specific security controls that Acme Inc. should prioritize implementing to mitigate these risks. Briefly explain how each control addresses the identified threats.

3. Implementation Challenges and Considerations:

Discuss potential challenges that Acme Inc. might face when implementing the recommended security controls. These challenges could be technical, financial, or resource related.

Suggest strategies for overcoming these challenges and ensuring successful implementation of the security controls.

Additional Considerations:

- Use relevant security terminology to demonstrate your understanding of the materials covered in Module 9.
- You may use external resources to support your explanations, but ensure all information is properly cited.
- Focus on providing practical recommendations that can be tailored to the specific needs of Acme Inc.
- Remember: There are no right or wrong answers here. The goal is to demonstrate your ability to apply your knowledge of sector-specific security standards to a real-world scenario.

By completing this workshop, you will gain valuable insights into the importance of aligning security practices with industry best practices and regulatory requirements. Conducting risk assessments to identify and prioritize security controls. Overcoming challenges associated with implementing security measures within an organization.

NOTES

MODULE 10.
MATURITY MODELS & PROFESSIONAL DEVELOPMENT

This module explores cybersecurity maturity models, professional development avenues, and ethical considerations. Gain insights into capability maturity models, career paths, industry certifications, ethical principles, skills development, and professional codes of conduct to elevate your cybersecurity expertise and align with industry best practices.

10.1 CYBERSECURITY CAPABILITY MATURITY MODELS (C2M2, ESSENTIAL 8 MATURITY MODEL)

Cybersecurity capability maturity models are frameworks designed to help organizations assess and improve their cybersecurity posture systematically. These models provide a structured approach to evaluating an organization's current security practices and identifying areas for improvement, enabling organizations to prioritize and implement effective cybersecurity measures tailored to their specific needs and risk profiles.

The Cybersecurity Capability Maturity Model (C2M2) is a widely recognized framework developed by the U.S. Department of Energy in collaboration with industry partners. It provides a comprehensive set of cybersecurity practices organized into 10 domains, each with specific objectives and maturity levels. The domains cover areas such as risk management, incident response, access control, and workforce management.

By assessing their current practices against the C2M2 model, organizations can determine their maturity level for each domain and develop a roadmap for improvement. The model defines four maturity levels. Partially Performed, Largely Performed, Fully Performed, and Continuously Improving. As organizations progress through these levels, they can establish a more robust and resilient cybersecurity program aligned with industry best practices.

The Essential Eight Maturity Model is another valuable framework developed by the Australian Cyber Security Centre (ACSC). It focuses specifically on the implementation and maturity of the ACSC's Essential Eight cybersecurity mitigation strategies. These strategies address critical areas such as application whitelisting, patching applications, restricting administrative privileges, and implementing multi-factor authentication.

The Essential Eight Maturity Model defines three maturity levels for each strategy. Maturity Level 1 (Partially Adhered), Maturity Level 2 (Largely Adhered), and Maturity Level 3 (Fully Complied). By assessing their maturity levels and implementing the recommended controls, organizations can significantly reduce their exposure to cyber threats and establish a strong cybersecurity foundation.

Utilizing capability maturity models offers several benefits to organizations:

1. **Structured approach**. These models provide a structured and systematic approach to assessing and improving cybersecurity practices, ensuring a comprehensive and consistent evaluation.
2. **Prioritization and resource allocation**. By identifying areas of weakness or low maturity, organizations can prioritize their efforts and allocate resources more effectively to address critical gaps.
3. **Benchmarking and continuous improvement**. Maturity models enable organizations to benchmark their cybersecurity posture against industry standards and establish a roadmap for continuous improvement.
4. **Regulatory compliance**. Many maturity models align with regulatory requirements and industry standards, helping organizations demonstrate compliance and adherence to best practices.

Incorporating cybersecurity capability maturity models into an organization's cybersecurity strategy promotes a proactive and structured approach to risk management, enabling organizations to enhance their overall cybersecurity resilience and effectively protect their critical assets and data.

10.2 CAREER PATHS AND CERTIFICATIONS IN CYBER SECURITY

The field of cybersecurity offers a wide range of career paths and opportunities for professionals with diverse skill sets and interests. As the demand for cybersecurity experts continues to grow, individuals can choose from various roles, including security analyst, penetration tester, incident responder, security architect, and chief information security officer (CISO).

To demonstrate their knowledge and expertise, many cybersecurity professionals pursue industry-recognized certifications. These certifications not only validate an individual's skills but also enhance their credibility and career advancement prospects. Some of the most widely recognized cybersecurity certifications include:

1. **Certified Information Systems Security Professional (CISSP)**. Offered by (ISC)^2, the CISSP is a globally recognized certification that covers a broad range of cybersecurity domains, including security and risk management, asset security, security architecture and engineering, and incident response.
2. **Certified Ethical Hacker (CEH).** Provided by the EC-Council, the CEH certification validates an individual's skills in identifying and mitigating security vulnerabilities through ethical hacking techniques.
3. **Certified Information Security Manager (CISM).** Offered by ISACA, the CISM certification focuses on information security governance, risk management, and compliance.
4. **Offensive Security Certified Professional (OSCP).** This certification, administered by Offensive Security, validates an individual's ability to perform advanced penetration testing and ethical hacking techniques.

5. **GIAC Security Certifications**. GIAC (Global Information Assurance Certification) offers a range of specialized certifications in areas such as incident response, penetration testing, security leadership, and industrial control systems security.

In addition to certifications, many educational institutions offer degree programs and specialized courses in cybersecurity, providing a solid foundation in the theoretical and practical aspects of the field.

Cybersecurity professionals can further enhance their careers by actively participating in industry events, conferences, and online communities, where they can network with peers, share knowledge, and stay updated on the latest trends and developments.

Continuous learning and professional development are essential in the rapidly evolving cybersecurity landscape. Professionals should embrace a lifelong learning mindset, as new threats and technologies emerge constantly, requiring them to adapt and acquire new skills continuously.

Overall, the cybersecurity field offers diverse and rewarding career paths for individuals with a passion for protecting digital assets and mitigating cyber risks. By pursuing relevant certifications, education, and professional development opportunities, cybersecurity professionals can unlock new career prospects, contribute to the security of organizations, and play a vital role in safeguarding critical systems and data.

10.3 ETHICAL PRINCIPLES AND CONSIDERATIONS

Ethical principles and considerations are fundamental to the practice of cybersecurity. As cybersecurity professionals gain access to sensitive information and possess the knowledge and tools to potentially cause harm, it is crucial to adhere to a strong ethical framework and uphold the highest standards of integrity and responsibility.

Some key ethical principles and considerations in cybersecurity include:

1. **Confidentiality, Integrity, and Availability (CIA Triad).** The CIA Triad is a core principle in cybersecurity, emphasizing the protection of confidential information, ensuring the integrity of data and systems, and maintaining their availability to authorized users.
2. **Privacy and Data Protection**. Cybersecurity professionals must respect individual privacy rights and ensure the proper handling and protection of personal and sensitive data in compliance with applicable laws and regulations.
3. **Responsible Disclosure**. When vulnerabilities or security flaws are discovered, cybersecurity professionals should follow responsible

disclosure practices, reporting the issues to the affected parties through proper channels before publicly disclosing them.

4. **Ethical Hacking and Penetration Testing**. Ethical hacking and penetration testing activities should only be conducted with explicit permission and within well-defined scopes and rules of engagement to avoid causing unintended harm or disruptions.

5. **Non-Maleficence**. The principle of non-maleficence dictates that cybersecurity professionals should avoid causing harm or engaging in activities that could lead to the exploitation or misuse of systems, networks, or data.

6. **Transparency and Accountability**. Cybersecurity professionals should maintain transparency in their actions and be accountable for their decisions and the potential consequences of their work.

7. **Professional Competence**. Continuously developing and maintaining professional competence through education, training, and staying up to date with the latest technologies and best practices is essential for ethical cybersecurity practice.

8. **Conflict of Interest**. Cybersecurity professionals should identify and address potential conflicts of interest that could compromise their objectivity, integrity, or ethical decision-making.

9. **Respect for Intellectual Property**. Cybersecurity activities should respect intellectual property rights and avoid unauthorized access, use, or distribution of proprietary information or software.

10. **Compliance with Laws and Regulations**. Cybersecurity professionals must ensure their actions comply with relevant laws, regulations, and organizational policies governing cyber activities, data protection, and privacy.

Ethical considerations in cybersecurity are not limited to technical aspects but also encompass broader societal and human implications. Cybersecurity professionals play a critical role in protecting digital assets and safeguarding the privacy and security of individuals and organizations. By upholding ethical principles and fostering a culture of ethics and integrity, cybersecurity professionals can build trust, maintain professionalism, and contribute to a more secure and responsible digital landscape.

10.4 CYBER SECURITY SKILLS DEVELOPMENT

Cyber security skills development is an ongoing and essential process for professionals in this rapidly evolving field. The cybersecurity landscape is constantly changing, with new threats, vulnerabilities, and technologies emerging regularly. As a result, cybersecurity professionals must continuously develop and enhance their skills to stay ahead of adversaries and effectively protect against cyber threats.

Effective cybersecurity skills development can involve several approaches:

1. **Formal education and training**. Many universities and educational institutions offer degree programs, certifications, and specialized courses in cybersecurity. These formal educational pathways provide a solid foundation in the theoretical and practical aspects of cybersecurity, covering topics such as network security, cryptography, risk management, and incident response.

2. **On-the-job training and mentorship**. Hands-on experience is invaluable in cybersecurity. Working under the guidance of experienced professionals, participating in projects, and tackling real-world scenarios can significantly contribute to skill development. Mentorship programs, where seasoned cybersecurity experts share their knowledge and insights, can also accelerate learning and skill acquisition.

3. **Self-study and online resources**. With the abundance of online resources, such as tutorials, blogs, webinars, and online communities, cybersecurity professionals can engage in self-study and continuously expand their knowledge. Online learning platforms and massive open online courses (MOOCs) offer flexible and affordable options for skill development.

4. **Cybersecurity competitions and challenges**. Participating in cybersecurity competitions and challenges, such as Capture the Flag (CTF) events and bug bounty programs, can provide practical experience in identifying and mitigating vulnerabilities, enhancing problem-solving skills, and fostering a competitive mindset.

5. **Professional certifications**. Obtaining industry-recognized certifications, such as the Certified Information Systems Security Professional (CISSP), Certified Ethical Hacker (CEH), or GIAC certifications, can validate an individual's knowledge and skills while demonstrating a commitment to professional development.

6. **Attending conferences and networking**. Attending cybersecurity conferences, workshops, and industry events can expose professionals to the latest trends, emerging technologies, and best practices. Networking with peers and experts in the field can also facilitate knowledge sharing and collaboration.

Effective cybersecurity skills development requires a combination of theoretical knowledge, practical experience, and a commitment to continuous learning. As cybersecurity threats and technologies evolve rapidly, professionals must stay proactive, adaptable, and dedicated to expanding their skills and expertise. By prioritizing skill development, cybersecurity professionals can enhance their effectiveness, contribute to stronger organizational security postures, and advance their careers in this dynamic and critical field.

10.5 PROFESSIONAL CODES OF CONDUCT

Professional codes of conduct in cybersecurity provide a set of guidelines and ethical principles that establish standards for behaviour and decision-making within the industry. These codes aim to promote professionalism, integrity, and responsible practices among cybersecurity professionals, fostering trust and ensuring the protection of critical systems and data.

Several organizations and professional bodies have developed codes of conduct specific to the cybersecurity field, including:

1. **(ISC)² Code of Ethics**. Developed by the International Information System Security Certification Consortium, commonly known as (ISC)², this code outlines principles such as protecting society, acting honourably, providing diligent and competent service, and advancing the profession.
2. **ISSA Code of Ethics.** The Information Systems Security Association (ISSA) has established a code of ethics that emphasizes integrity, objectivity, professional competence, confidentiality, and respect for the legitimate interests of others.
3. **ISACA Code of Professional Ethics**. The Information Systems Audit and Control Association (ISACA) has a code that requires members to act with integrity, due care, and professionalism while upholding the confidentiality and privacy of information.
4. **EC-Council Code of Ethics**. The International Council of E-Commerce Consultants (EC-Council) has a code that focuses on ethical hacking practices, responsible disclosure, and respecting intellectual property rights.
5. **SANS Code of Ethics. The SANS** Institute has developed a code that emphasizes professional conduct, technical excellence, honesty, and the protection of society's digital assets.

These codes of conduct typically address several key areas, including:

1. **Integrity and professional conduct**. Cybersecurity professionals are expected to act with honesty, objectivity, and ethical behaviour, avoiding conflicts of interest and upholding the highest standards of professional conduct.
2. **Confidentiality and data protection**. Protecting sensitive information, maintaining client confidentiality, and ensuring the privacy and security of data are paramount responsibilities outlined in these codes.
3. **Responsible and lawful practices**. Cybersecurity activities must be conducted within the bounds of applicable laws, regulations, and organizational policies, while respecting intellectual property rights and avoiding unauthorized access or harm.
4. **Competence and continuous learning**. Cybersecurity professionals are encouraged to maintain and enhance their knowledge and skills through continuous education and training, staying up-to-date with the latest developments in the field.
5. **Respect and social responsibility**. These codes often emphasize the importance of respecting the rights and legitimate interests of others, as

well as promoting the responsible use of technology for the benefit of society.

By adhering to professional codes of conduct, cybersecurity professionals demonstrate their commitment to ethical practices, accountability, and the protection of critical assets and data. These codes serve as guiding principles, fostering trust among clients, organizations, and the broader community, while upholding the integrity and reputation of the cybersecurity profession.

10.6 WORKSHOP EXERCISE: CYBERSECURITY MATURITY MODELS & PROFESSIONAL DEVELOPMENT

Workshop Exercise - Skills Development for Acme Inc.

Scenario: Imagine you are a cybersecurity consultant working for a consulting firm. You are assigned to Acme Inc., a leading manufacturer of industrial robots used in various industries. Acme Inc. is experiencing significant growth and is expanding its operations globally. They are aware of the importance of cybersecurity and have requested your expertise in developing a comprehensive skills development plan for their IT and security teams.

Instructions: This workshop can be completed individually or in groups of 2-4 students. Please submit a written report of your findings in the designated Workshop document downloaded from the Assignments folder (400 words maximum).

Your report should address the following aspects:

1. Skills Gap Analysis:

Conduct a high-level skills gap analysis for Acme Inc.'s IT and security teams. Consider the current skill sets of your team members, the evolving cybersecurity landscape, and the specific security needs of Acme Inc.'s industrial robot manufacturing operations. Identify key cybersecurity skill gaps that need to be addressed.

2. Training and Development Recommendations:

Based on the identified skills gaps, recommend specific training and development programs to address the needs of Acme Inc.'s IT and security teams. Consider various training formats like instructor-led courses, online training platforms, certification programs, and mentorship opportunities.

3. Implementation and Evaluation:

Propose methods for evaluating the effectiveness of the training programs to ensure they are meeting the desired learning outcomes and contributing to a more skilled and knowledgeable security team.

4. Continuous Learning Culture:

Recommend strategies to promote continuous learning, such as knowledge sharing initiatives, internal workshops, and participation in industry conferences and events.

Additional Considerations:

- Use relevant security terminology to demonstrate your understanding of the materials covered in Module 10.
- You may use external resources to support your explanations, but ensure all information is properly cited.
- Focus on providing practical recommendations that can be tailored to the specific needs of Acme Inc.
- Remember: There are no right or wrong answers here. The goal is to demonstrate your ability to apply your knowledge of cybersecurity skills development to a real-world scenario.

By completing this workshop, you will gain valuable insights into:

- Conducting skills gap analysis to identify training needs within a cybersecurity team.
- Developing a comprehensive training and development plan for cybersecurity professionals.
- Implementing and evaluating training programs to ensure effectiveness.

Fostering a culture of continuous learning within a cybersecurity team.

NOTES

www.ingramcontent.com/pod-product-compliance
Lightning Source LLC
LaVergne TN
LVHW081759050326
832903LV00027B/2021